Joycelyn Edwards

The HIM BOOK

The HIM BOOK

Where the Sermon and Song Meet at the Foot of the Cross

Dr. John R. Adolph

Townsend Press
Nashville, Tennessee

This book is dedicated to Jesus Christ, Lord and Savior of the world.

Table of Contents

Acknowledgments

As the administrator for the Inheritance Conference 2021, I have been blessed to work with some of the most wonderful people in the Kingdom of our God: pastors, preachers, psalmists, prayer warriors, administrators, administrative assistants, coordinators, graphic artists, photographers, videographers, back-office tech personnel—and the list goes on. A conference of this magnitude requires so many people to make it come to fruition with excellence until the list of people to thank is inexhaustible for me. However, an acknowledgment section like this one is a noteworthy Christian gesture for an outstanding work as *The HIM BOOK*.

I wish to take a moment of total honesty and transparency as I begin to express my gratitude to all who helped this work develop from conception to completion. When Pastor Adolph mentioned the words "Christocentric anthology" to me, I had no idea what he was talking about. More than that, when he told me that he planned to get twenty-two of the nation's busiest Pastors to write an article for this book and submit it to him, I thought he was losing his mind. I gave him a blank stare as he sat there, filled with excitement about this project. And week after week, I watched the Lord send article after article into my office.

With this in mind, I would like to thank God for my team that helped me pull this book together. Thanks go to Reverend Alfred Beverly, Michael Allen, James Ural, and Ri'Keam Kenebrew for their labor, time, and commitment. I praise the Lord for the partnership of the Executive Staff of Antioch Missionary Baptist Church, who often work behind the scenes making sure that all goes well. To you guys, I say, "Thanks for your support." I must thank the Lord for the publisher of this work, who stepped in with a contract and got everything moving in the right direction. I sincerely appreciate you, Dr. Derrick Jackson; I'm forever indebted to you. I must praise God for the editors, proofreaders, and layout/design artists. Without you, this book would not look like it does today.

Next, I would like to thank the twenty-two Pastors who took the time to work with my office to complete this entire book. I appreciate each of you in a very special way. I want to extend thanks to Lady Dorrie, Sumone, and Jonathan for allowing Pastor the time to work the works of the one that sent him to us while it is day. I sincerely appreciate and applaud you, Pastor Adolph (JRA), for the vision, hard work, and tireless hours you give others every day of your life and for trusting me with projects of this magnitude. My prayer is always to please the Lord and make you proud.

Lastly, I want to thank Jesus Christ, who is my personal Lord and Savior. I had no idea that I would ever partner in publishing such a marvelous work about HIM. Not to mention, I was blessed to design the logo for this book after Pastor told me what he had in mind. Yet, through the leadership of the Holy Spirit and the working hands of many, you now hold in your possession the HIM BOOK. It is the place where the sermon and the song meet at the foot of the Cross. Thank You, Jesus, for Your finished work and special thanks to everyone who worked to make this book come to pass.

Minister Brooklyn D. Williams,
Executive Director of John R. Adolph Ministries
IC 2021 Conference Administrator

Introduction

Not long ago, I prayerfully sought the Lord on the subject matter for a new series to teach the Antioch church and could sense the pressing of the Holy Spirit to lead the flock over which He has given me charge about "Him." To empower my study and enhance my substance, I walked into a neighboring Christian bookstore and asked an attendant for a good book about "Him"—to which the attendant said, "All we have for that kind of study is the Bible." I quickly agreed that the Bible would, of course, be the root reference material to guide my study, but I wanted a book that would take the titles given for Jesus Christ in the Scriptures and teach me what each of them meant. To my surprise, the clerk in the store politely told me, "We don't carry a book like that." When I heard this, I was astonished beyond description.

I took a stroll around the bookstore and took note of the plenteous books. There were books for almost everything, but no existing book presented Jesus Christ in type, symbol, and direct statement. No one book would take the titles of Jesus Christ and teach them with clarity, simplicity, doctrinal soundness, and godly integrity. Thus, the genesis of this project started its spiritual formulation. When I returned to my humble abode, I sat and prayerfully decided that instead of looking for a book of this magnitude, I would work diligently with some of the greatest theological minds of our day to produce it. Thus, the information shared in this book would be for the Christocentric growth of Disciples of Jesus around the world to utilize.

Thus, the purpose of this work is not to set forth some theological treatise that will serve as a platform of debate in days to come, even though this document does contain theology. This work is not an exegetical reprise produced for systematic theologians to grapple along the circumference of its depth—though it does indeed hold a degree of systematic theology. This text is not a hymn book, filled with songs whose lyrics are rooted in doctrinal truth—yet the book will contain the great hymns of the church. This book is a Christological anthology whose sole purpose is to take the titles of Jesus Christ ascribed to Him in the Scriptures and have the most phenomenal pastors of our age share "Him" with the world—and celebrate Him with great hymns that move the human heart with His redemptive love expressed at Calvary. In short, this book is where the sermon and the song meet at the foot of the Cross.

This work will present six significant shifts per chapter: (1) the author, (2) the Christocentric title and passage, (3) the great hymn of the church, (4) a moment of prayer bearing the title "Now Unto Him," followed by (5) the essay and concluding with (6) another great hymn of the church. Welcome to the first-ever HIM Book!

The HIM BOOK

DR. DAVE ANDERSON
Grace School of Theology
Houston, Texas

DR. DAVE ANDERSON
GRACE SCHOOL OF THEOLOGY
HOUSTON, TEXAS

JESUS IS THE SON OF GOD

Hebrews 1:1-14

1 God, who at sundry times and in divers manners spake in time past unto the fathers by the prophets,

2 Hath in these last days spoken unto us by his Son, whom he hath appointed heir of all things, by whom also he made the worlds;

3 Who being the brightness of his glory, and the express image of his person, and upholding all things by the word of his power, when he had by himself purged our sins, sat down on the right hand of the Majesty on high:

4 Being made so much better than the angels, as he hath by inheritance obtained a more excellent name than they.

5 For unto which of the angels said he at any time, Thou art my Son, this day have I begotten thee? And again, I will be to him a Father, and he shall be to me a Son?

6 And again, when he bringeth in the firstbegotten into the world, he saith, And let all the angels of God worship him.

7 And of the angels he saith, Who maketh his angels spirits, and his ministers a flame of fire.

8 But unto the Son he saith, Thy throne, O God, is for ever and ever: a sceptre of righteousness is the sceptre of thy kingdom.

9 Thou hast loved righteousness, and hated iniquity; therefore God, even thy God, hath anointed thee with the oil of gladness above thy fellows.

10 And, Thou, Lord, in the beginning hast laid the foundation of the earth; and the heavens are the works of thine hands:

11 They shall perish; but thou remainest; and they all shall wax old as doth a garment;

12 And as a vesture shalt thou fold them up, and they shall be changed: but thou art the same, and thy years shall not fail.

13 But to which of the angels said he at any time, Sit on my right hand, until I make thine enemies thy footstool?

14 Are they not all ministering spirits, sent forth to minister for them who shall be heirs of salvation?

THE GREAT HYMN
THE BATTLE HYMN OF THE REPUBLIC

Mine eyes have seen the glory of the coming of the Lord
He is trampling out the vintage where the grapes
of wrath are stored
He has loosed the fateful lightening of
His terrible swift sword

His truth is marching on (gloria)
Glory, glory, hallelujah (gloria)
Glory, glory, hallelujah (gloria, gloria)
Glory, glory, hallelujah (gloria)
His truth is marching on

I have seen Him in the watch-fires of a hundred circling
camps They have builded Him an altar in the evening dews
and damps I can read His righteous sentence in the dim and
flaring lamps His day is marching on

Glory, glory, hallelujah Glory, glory, hallelujah Glory glory
hallelujah His truth is marching on
In the beauty of the lilies Christ was born across the sea
With a glory in His bosom that transfigures you and me As He
died to make men holy let us live to make men free
While God is marching on

Glory, glory, hallelujah
Glory, glory, hallelujah
Glory glory hallelujah
His truth is marching on

Glory, glory, hallelujah
Glory, glory, hallelujah
Glory glory hallelujah
His truth is marching on, amen, amen

All-wise and eternal God, I approach You at this moment, aware of Your holiness, Your righteousness, and Your kindness. I bow in submission to Your ability, integrity, and ubiquity. My sacred supplication to lay at Your feet is to praise You for who You are in the heavens and what You are in the earth. You are the Son of God, and for this cause I honor, praise, lift, adore, bless, exalt, and magnify You. In the name of He who died and rose again I pray. Amen.

Article 1

**THE GREAT HIM
JESUS IS THE SON OF GOD
Hebrews 1:1-14**

**by
Dr. Dave Anderson**

As Christmas is approaching, we will begin to hear beloved Christmas carols like "O, Little Town of Bethlehem," "Silent Night," and "Away in a Manger." One of those melodies asks a question and attempts an answer, but the answer is incomplete: "What Child is This?" The carol answers, "This is Christ the King . . . the Babe, the Son of Mary." Of course, this is true—but not the full answer. We find that answer in Hebrews 1. The answer is in the ring structure of Hebrews 1. For each claim about Jesus in Hebrews 1:1-4, there is a corresponding OT quote to support that claim in Hebrews 1:5-14.

The first ring starts with a statement of His Exaltation—"heir of all things"—this happened after His ascension, when He sat down at the right hand of His Father. Then the author moves back in time to the Creation and claims that Jesus was the Creator—"through whom He also made the worlds." Now the writer goes even further back in time to before Creation to make a claim for the Deity of Christ—"express image of His person." But then the author moves forward in time to the created order to claim that Jesus is holding all of creation together. He is the Sustainer—"upholding all things by the word of His power" (verse 3). Then he comes full circle by returning to His Exaltation: "He . . . sat down at the right hand of the Majesty on high, being made so much better than the angels, as he hath by inheritance obtained a more excellent name than they" (verses 3-4). From heir (verse 2) to an heir (verse 4)—a full circle or ring. But now, he supports these claims, point by point, from the OT. What Child is This?

He is the EXALTED ONE. "You are my Son, today I have begotten You" (verse 5, ESV). There were three phases to the Sonship of Christ: the Son in eternity past, the Son after His baptism and during His ministry, and the Son by adoption after His ascension. This third phase was a reward given to a faithful servant by a king. Jesus, the Suffering Servant (see Isaiah 52:13–53:12), lived a perfectly faithful life. In the Ancient Near East, a faithful servant was adopted to be a son and given a reward—usually a land piece. The almighty King adopted

5

Three elements that makes God God : Time, Space and Matter

His faithful servant to be His Son: "I will be to him a Father, and he shall be to me a Son." His reward? Planet Earth during His one-thousand-year reign. We can't underestimate the importance of His "better name." No where do we find the name "Jesus" or "Christ" in this chapter. It was "Son." But we have only begun to answer our question.

He is the CREATOR. Scientists like to talk about the "Big Bang." String theorists think we have eleven or more dimensions, which remains to be seen. But we know for sure about four: length, width, height, and time. Time needs a beginning. *Time* is defined as cause and effect. We believe that the initial, efficient reason was Jesus, the Son, Prime Mover (cause) who began this universe. Jesus was the cause; the universe was the effect. Support? As in the first ring, we are going back in time. In fact, we are going to the beginning of time . . . if we define time as cause and effect. The first cause was the creation of the angels before creating our universe (see Job 38:4-7). Here, the Son "maketh his angels spirits, and his ministers a flame of fire." The spiritual universe existed before the physical universe. What Child is This? He's the **EXALTED ONE** and the **CREATOR**. But that's not all. He is also . . .

GOD. Now we go even further back—back before time, before any cause and effect. In the first ring, the Son had the exact same essence, image, and attributes. For OT support, we go to the only passage in the Bible that explicitly calls Him God—"Of the Son he says, 'Your throne, O God, is forever and ever'" (verse 8, ESV). So, who is this? He's the **EXALTED ONE,** the **CREATOR,** and the **VERY GOD.** But wait a minute. Let's not stop there. He is the . . .

SUSTAINER. In the first ring, we read, "[He upholds] all things by the word of his power [or His powerful word]" (verse 9). There are four forces we know about in our universe. The strongest of these keeps the nucleus together. The nucleus contains only positive charges: protons (neutrons have no charge) like charges repel. The nucleus should blow apart. Why doesn't it? Because of the strong force that scientists call "gluon." Talk about superglue! But we know it is Jesus, the Son. He upholds all things. But in the second ring, we are moving forward in time to when He lets go—"Like a cloak You will fold them up" (verse 12, NKJV). The time for folding up has not yet come, but it will. "He knows when to hold 'em and He knows when to fold 'em." He is the **EXALTED ONE,** the **CREATOR,** the **VERY GOD,** and the **SUSTAINER.** But we aren't done. He is also . . .

HEIR. He inherited a better name (Son) than the angels in verse 4 when He sat down by His Father. Now the writer draws on Psalm 110 for support: "Sit at My right hand, till I make

Your enemies Your footstool" (verse 1, NKJV). He looks to the time when the Son will rule over the entire earth.

What Child is This? He is the **EXALTED ONE,** the **CREATOR,** the **VERY GOD,** the **SUSTAINER,** and the **HEIR** of all things. What Child is This? He is the **SON**. And now He wants to lead many sons to glory (2:10). That's the theme of the book. The last three chapters are "The Search for Faithful Sons." He wants you and me to be more than children. He wants us to grow up to become sons (see Hebrews 5:12-14). Those who are sons and co-heirs with the Firstborn will be revealed when He returns (see Romans 8:19). Until then, let us bow down before the **EXALTED ONE,** the **CREATOR,** the **VERY GOD,** the **SUSTAINER,** and the **HEIR** of all things. So, I think we have answered the question, **"What Child is This?"** But wait a minute? We have not responded to the question, **"Why?"** Why did the Creator of the Cosmos become the Babe of Bethlehem? Why? Why would God so humble Himself to do this? It's right here. It is in chapter 1. It's in the rings. I just read right over it. Something is in the first ring that is not in the second ring. Something is conspicuous by its absence in the second ring that is in the first ring.

What is it? What did I slide over? "When he had by himself purged our sins" (verse 3c). That's not in the second ring. That's only in the first one. The rings tell us **what,** but the purification tells us **why.** You see, "Houston, we have a problem." The Bible calls it "sin." Only Christianity offers the exalted Son to get rid of our egregious sin. Yes, He is the **EXALTED ONE,** the **CREATOR,** the **VERY GOD,** the **SUSTAINER,** and the **HEIR** of all things. But He is also the **PURIFIER,** whose blood washes the sin away for anyone who believes in Him and what He has done. Oh, come . . . let us believe in Him; oh, come . . . let us adore Him. The EXALTED ONE, the CREATOR, the VERY GOD, the SUSTAINER, and the HEIR of all things. And the **PURIFIER** from sin.

THE GREAT HYMN
AMAZING GRACE

Amazing grace
How sweet the sound
That saved a wretch like me I once was lost
But now I'm found
Was blind, but now I see

'Twas grace that taught
My heart to fear
And grace my Fears relieved How precious
did That grace appear
The hour I first believed

Through many dangers Toils and snares
We have already come 'Twas grace hath
brought Us safe thus far
And grace will lead us home

When we've been there
Ten thousand years
Bright shining as the sun
We'll have no less days to sing God's
praise Than when we first begun

Amazing grace
How sweet the sound
That saved a wretch like me I once was lost
But now I'm found
Was blind, but now I see

PASTOR TERRY K. ANDERSON
Lilly Grove Missionary Baptist Church
Houston, Texas

PASTOR TERRY K. ANDERSON
LILLY GROVE MISSIONARY BAPTIST CHURCH
HOUSTON, TEXAS

JESUS IS THE CHIEF CORNERSTONE

Psalm 118:1-22

1 O give thanks unto the Lord; for he is good: because his mercy endureth for ever.

2 Let Israel now say, that his mercy endureth for ever.

3 Let the house of Aaron now say, that his mercy endureth for ever.

4 Let them now that fear the Lord say, that his mercy endureth for ever.

5 I called upon the Lord in distress: the Lord answered me, and set me in a large place.

6 The Lord is on my side; I will not fear: what can man do unto me?

7 The Lord taketh my part with them that help me: therefore shall I see my desire upon them that hate me.

8 It is better to trust in the Lord than to put confidence in man.

9 It is better to trust in the Lord than to put confidence in princes.

10 All nations compassed me about: but in the name of the Lord will I destroy them.

11 They compassed me about; yea, they compassed me about: but in the name of the Lord I will destroy them.

12 They compassed me about like bees: they are quenched as the fire of thorns: for in the name of the Lord I will destroy them.

13 Thou hast thrust sore at me that I might fall: but the Lord helped me.

14 The Lord is my strength and song, and is become my salvation.

15 The voice of rejoicing and salvation is in the tabernacles of the righteous: the right hand of the Lord doeth valiantly.

16 The right hand of the Lord is exalted: the right hand of the Lord doeth valiantly.

17 I shall not die, but live, and declare the works of the Lord.

18 The Lord hath chastened me sore: but he hath not given me over unto death.

19 Open to me the gates of righteousness: I will go into them, and I will praise the Lord:

20 This gate of the Lord, into which the righteous shall enter.

21 I will praise thee: for thou hast heard me, and art become my salvation.

22 The stone which the builders refused is become the head stone of the corner.

THE GREAT HYMN
I GO TO THE ROCK

Where do I go when there's nobody else to turn to?
Who do I talk to when nobody wants to listen?
Who do I lean on when there's no foundation stable?
I go to the rock
I know he's able
I go to the rock
I go to the rock for my salvation
I go to the stone that the builders rejected
I run to the mountain and the mountain stands by me
When the Earth all around me is sinking sand
On Christ, the solid rock I stand
When I need a shelter, when I need a friend
I go to the rock
Where do I go, where do I go
When the storms of life are threatening?
Who do I turn to when those winds of sorrow blow?
And is there a refuge in the time of tribulation?
I go to the rock
I know He's able
I go to the rock
I know He's the rock for my salvation
I know He's the stone that the builders rejected
I run to the mountain and the mountain stands by me
When the Earth all around me is sinking sand
On Christ, the solid rock I stand
When I need a shelter, when I need a friend
I go to the rock
I know He's the rock for my salvation
I know He's the stone that the builders rejected
I run to the mountain and the mountain stands by me
When the Earth all around me is sinking sand
On Christ, the solid rock I stand
When I need a shelter, when I need a friend

In times like these, O Lord, there seems to be nothing stable. In seasons like these, O God, there appears to be nothing trustworthy. However, in the depths of my eternal soul, I know that You are there. From the essence of my frail human existence, I whisper these mere words to You, and I hope that they bring a smile upon Your face as You sit governing the galaxy— You are my rock. In Jesus' name I pray. Amen.

God deserves space and time in your life.

1. Rejected Due to Alignment
2. Rejected Due to Allotment
3. Rejected Due to Assignment

Article 2

THE GREAT HIM
JESUS IS THE CHIEF CORNERSTONE
Psalm 118:1-22

by
Pastor Terry K. Anderson

Although a great deal of uncertainty abounds concerning the writing of Psalm 118, some would include it among the post-exilic collection of reports, perhaps written by David, Hezekiah, Isaiah, Nehemiah, Zechariah, or Haggai. It is the last of the Hallel psalms (113–118) and was usually sung at the conclusion of the Paschal Feast. Psalm 118 is not only messianic and prophetic, but also it is liturgical, arranged antiphonally for the Feast of Tabernacles. As the worshipers drew near to the gates of the Temple, they proclaimed the miracle of God's magnificent deliverance of His people.

This psalm is also what Dr. John Phillips, retired assistant director of Moody Correspondence School and Bible commentator, calls "an envelope psalm." With this in mind, the first verse commences with praise to God for His amazing goodness and grace and also closes with the same words: "O give thanks unto the LORD; for He is good: because His mercy endureth for ever." Between the simple prayer in verses 19-21 and the sounding praise of verses 24-26 is the sudden pause in verse 22, which is the verse under consideration in this pericope: "The stone which the builders refused is become the head stone of the corner." That stone, conspicuously despised, is now conspicuously displayed.

There are six references to this statement in the New Testament, three of which were made by the Lord Jesus Himself. In Acts 4:11, Peter quoted this Scripture when he and John were arrested by the Sanhedrin for healing the lame man and preaching in the Name of Jesus. The cornerstone is the principal stone around which all construction in antiquity was achieved. In the lexicon of biblical images of architecture, no image is more evocative than the cornerstone—the focal point of a building, the thing on which it most depends for structural integrity. Thus, in one of the oldest books in the Bible, God's voice asks from the whirlwind in Job 38:6 regarding the Creation, "Who laid [its] corner stone?"

HE's The Head because He:
1. Reveals The Future
2. Reveals The Facts
3. Reveals The Father

The HIM BOOK

The Corner stone
keeps every, holds
everything and
maintains everything

As aforementioned, the date of the writing and the authorship of the psalm is unknown, as is the original meaning of the text. However, the Aramaic phrase of the Targum, which is a paraphrase or interpretation of the Hebrew Bible, clearly understands the passage in a royal sense: "The young man which the builders abandoned is among the sons of Jesse and is worthy to be appointed to kingship and rule." The cornerstone image is further amplified by the references to the "stone of stumbling" and "Rock of Offense" images from Isaiah. The combination of the passages from Isaiah and Psalm 118:22 links the early Church's understanding of faith with its emerging Christology: faith in Christ makes Him a tried stone—a precious cornerstone—while unbelief makes Him a stone of stumbling.

Not only are stones called upon to be a witness (as in Joshua 24:27), but also, in the New Testament, Paul draws on the temple-building metaphor in Ephesians 2:20-21 to construct his famous vision of the Church, "built upon the foundation of the apostles and prophets, with Christ Jesus himself as the cornerstone. In him the whole structure is joined together and grows into a holy temple in the Lord" (NRSV). The verse may now be illustrated by a reference to Christ in offices that only Jesus is worthy to occupy: Prophet, Priest, and King.

As a Prophet, the Son bears such relation to the Father as speech does to thought. As the Law from Mount Sinai and worshipped on Mount Zion, when the Messiah came in human form, the Jewish builders' anger was excited. They were so enthusiastic over His claims of being God that He became the stone that the builders rejected—and yet, though rejected, He has become the head of the corner. And to prove Himself the Faithful and True Witness, He rose from the dead and is now exalted as the great Prophet of the Church.

As a Priest, the ordination of Jesus is eternal. In the Aaronic and Levitical priesthoods, the office remained as long as the sacerdotal dignity was vested in the living person. They performed their duties continuously for the sins of the people and when their day was done, so also was their priesthood. But when Christ died at Calvary, He not only offered a sacrifice but also became the sacrifice so that grace could provide what holiness demanded. Unlike the priests of the Old Testament, who perpetually sacrificed without the dignity of ever being seated, He made His sacrifice once for all and is not now standing at the right hand of God because that would make Him a Servant; He is not now kneeling at the right hand of God because that would make Him a slave, but He is now seated at the right hand of God—which makes Him a Son!

There's Nobody Quite Like Him

As a King, the incarnate Jesus often had been depicted by the prophets as a monarch—"on the throne of His father David"—yet "when He came to His own, His own received Him not" (see John 1:11). Who could fancy a king who wore no diadem and waved no banner, lived in obscurity and privation from a poor family and a place between nowhere and goodbye called Nazareth, and died in desertion and ignominy? But the stone, though disallowed of men, is chosen of God and precious. God has raised Him from the dead, placed Him at His right hand, and endowed Him with a universal government.

He is "the Stone" in the way of eminence and excellency. He is the matchless and incomparable Stone, for He is the chief Stone of the corner; the brightness of His Father's glory in Him, and the express image of the Godhead bodily. According to John, He is our Advocate, Lamb of God, the Resurrection and the Life. Peter names Him the Shepherd and Bishop of our Souls. Solomon calls Him our Rose of Sharon and Lily of the Valley. Isaiah says He is our Prince of Peace, and the Revelation calls Him the Lion of the Tribe of Judah and the Bright Morning Star. The rejected stone is Who He says He is.

1. He is Enthroned as Diety.

2.

3. He is Empowered with Majesty

15

THE GREAT HYMN
IN TIMES LIKE THESE

In times like these you need a Savior
In times like these you need an anchor
Be very sure, be very sure
Your anchor holds and grips the Solid Rock!
This Rock is Jesus, Yes He's the One
This Rock is Jesus, the only One
Be very sure, be very sure
Your anchor holds and grips the Solid Rock!

In times like these you need the Bible
In times like these, O be not idle
Be very sure, be very sure
Your anchor holds and grips the Solid Rock!
This Rock is Jesus, Yes He's the One
This Rock is Jesus, the only One
Be very sure, be very sure
Your anchor holds and grips the Solid Rock!

In times like these I have a Savior
In times like these I have an anchor
I'm very sure, I'm very sure
My anchor holds and grips the Solid Rock!
This Rock is Jesus, Yes He's the One
This Rock is Jesus, the only One
Be very sure, be very sure
Your anchor holds and grips the Solid Rock!

DR. JAMAL H. BRYANT
New Birth Missionary Baptist Church
Lithonia, Georgia

DR. JAMAL H. BRYANT
NEW BIRTH MISSIONARY BAPTIST CHURCH
LITHONIA, GEORGIA

JESUS IS EMMANUEL

Matthew 1:18-23

18 Now the birth of Jesus Christ was on this wise: When as his mother Mary was espoused to Joseph, before they came together, she was found with child of the Holy Ghost.

19 Then Joseph her husband, being a just man, and not willing to make her a public example, was minded to put her away privily.

20 But while he thought on these things, behold, the angel of the LORD appeared unto him in a dream, saying, Joseph, thou son of David, fear not to take unto thee Mary thy wife: for that which is conceived in her is of the Holy Ghost.

21 And she shall bring forth a son, and thou shalt call his name JESUS: for he shall save his people from their sins.

22 Now all this was done, that it might be fulfilled which was spoken of the Lord by the prophet, saying,

23 Behold, a virgin shall be with child, and shall bring forth a son, and they shall call his name Emmanuel, which being interpreted is, God with us.

THE GREAT HYMN
O COME, O COME EMMANUEL

O come, o come Emmanuel
To free your captive Israel
That mourns in lonely exile here
Until the Son of God appear
Rejoice, rejoice o Israel
To you shall come Emmanuel

O Lord, our Lord, how excellent is Thy name in all the earth. As I approach Your throne at this very moment, Your majesty is evident, Your sovereignty reigns, Your glory is too much for my heart to contain; nevertheless, I kneel because You sit. I bless You, O Lord, because Your most unique expression of love toward me was to become me to save me. I know, realize, and celebrate that when Jesus was born in Bethlehem of Judea, He was more than some baby born in a cow trough. He was God wrapped in a body. Emmanuel would be His name. Thank You, O Lord, for being God with me forever. In the name of Jesus I pray. Amen.

5-27-21-Thursday

He's With Us

1. We Cannot Lose
2. We Will Win
3. We Shall Overcome

6-3-21-Thursday

HE'S Not Having It

1. HE's Against Satan
2. HE Is Against Sinister People
3.

The HIM BOOK

Article 3

THE GREAT HIM
JESUS IS EMMANUEL
Matthew 1:18-23

"WE ARE IN THIS THING TOGETHER"

by
Dr. Jamal H. Bryant

Invariably every checkout counter in America—whether Target, Walmart, or the supermarket—has hoisted right above the chewing gum, *US Weekly* magazine. A gossip publication that's been in circulation since 1977 makes interesting observations. It focuses on celebrities' lives, reporting on the relationships, pregnancies, and the mundane activities of Hollywood's elite. Amazingly even in the digital age, they can unload one million copies a week. Part of their success strategy is psychology, which neither *People Magazine*, the *Enquirer*, nor TMZ employ, connects the average citizen with the celebrity just by using one word, US, which denotes inclusion and association. So, they'll show pictures of Cardi B eating a hamburger because that's US, they will publish Chadwick Boseman's family grieving at the funeral because that's US, they'll do articles about Oprah struggling with her weight because that's US.

In my previous life, before pastoring, I was national youth and college director of the NAACP. My job was mobilizing college students for advocacy and training for leadership. One of the programs I stumbled upon at Cal-Polytechnic Institute was called WITH US. This was a national bystander intervention research center committed to addressing critical social issues impacting college students' health, safety, and success. It was developed by the parents of a young man who died of alcohol poisoning during a hazing incident in a room full of people. It shed light on the fact that, in fact, the campus had no sense of community—thus making the environment ripe for rapes, robbery, and ratchetness.

Emma Lazarus, the Jewish poet and activist who is credited as having written the words inscribed at the base of the Statue of Liberty, "give me your tired, give me your poor yearning to breathe free." But her quote that rocked the civil rights community and wedded them to holocaust survivors was, "none of us are free until all of us are free." One group felt it in Germany, and another group faced it in Georgia, but it's still US.

The once-popular teen show *Mean Girls* reached an occult-like following from one scene. It was where a young lady whose hair was just casually done and whose clothes were not embedded with designer labels approached a table in the cafeteria. With a condescending glance, a group of popular girls announced dismissively, "You can't sit with us!"—thereby tearing a blood-stained page out of America's tattered history on segregation. It has been and remains a divided nation; where you sit, where you drink water, where you use the restroom, where you shop, and even where you worship often defines where you are socially accepted. The failing of America is not to realize we are in this thing together.

If you are not with us, then you are against us. Who is the US? If God be for US, then who can be against US? The whole notion of US rings familiar ordinarily when we get to the Advent season! It was foretold that His name shall be called Emmanuel, which translates to "God with us!" It's been widely accepted that Immanuel was given to a child during the time of King Ahaz; it was a sign that the children of God would be getting a reprieve from all the attacks they had endured. We had to wrestle; now we get to rest. We are in this thing together. Not to be glossed over is the fact that the child was the sign. In this era that we now occupy, what are our children the sign of?

His being with us is reminiscent of His manifested presence as punctuated in Exodus 13: "And the LORD went before them by day in a pillar of cloud, to lead them the way; and by night in a pillar of fire" (verse 21). In the spirit of Emmanuel I say, "Precious Lord, take my hand, lead me on and let me stand." He's with us! Before the Savior's ascension, He extended a promise to His devotees in Matthew 28:20b: "Lo, I am with you always, even unto the end of the world."

America was riveted to its core on June 17, 2015, in Charleston, South Carolina, when a historic church nestled downtown had converged for Bible study; only thirteen people had shown up in the fellowship hall. One of them was a first-time visitor by the name of Dylann Roof. When the session concluded, he calmly went to his car, returned with artillery, and unloaded his weapon, leaving nine dead—making it the largest execution in a house of worship. This incident glued me to the television, as it did everyone else. Emerging from the discharged shells, the yellow tape, and the army of media were three survivors. It was only then that I saw the sign behind them: Emmanuel!

God is with us when we are thrown into situations that we otherwise should not have survived. God is with us when we are clear that, quite frankly, we should have died—and God is with us in the moments when we want to go and hide. I am glad there was not just one survivor, or else the tense would have changed.

I have identical twin girls named Angel and Adore. The other night, I called Adore and asked to speak to her sister, to which she reported that her sister was away on a play date. I inquired innocently how she felt about her twin's being away with somebody else. She retorted, "God is not just with me, neither is God just with my sister. God is big enough to be with us both!" Remember this: nothing shall separate us from the love of God—for our favor lies in knowing that He is with US.

THE GREAT HYMN
GOD WILL TAKE CARE OF YOU

Mine eyes have seen the glory of the coming of the Lord
He is trampling out the vintage where the grapes
of wrath are stored
He has loosed the fateful lightening of
His terrible swift sword

His truth is marching on (gloria)
Glory, glory, hallelujah (gloria)
Glory, glory, hallelujah (gloria, gloria)
Glory, glory, hallelujah (gloria)
His truth is marching on

I have seen Him in the watch-fires of a hundred circling
camps They have builded Him an altar in the evening dews
and damps I can read His righteous sentence in the dim and
flaring lamps His day is marching on

Glory, glory, hallelujah Glory, glory, hallelujah Glory glory
hallelujah His truth is marching on
In the beauty of the lilies Christ was born across the sea
With a glory in His bosom that transfigures you and me As He
died to make men holy let us live to make men free
While God is marching on

Glory, glory, hallelujah
Glory, glory, hallelujah
Glory glory hallelujah
His truth is marching on

Glory, glory, hallelujah
Glory, glory, hallelujah
Glory glory hallelujah
His truth is marching on, amen, amen

DR. KENNETH G. CAMPBELL
Household of Faith Community Church
Houston, Texas

DR. KENNETH G. CAMPBELL
HOUSEHOLD OF FAITH COMMUNITY CHURCH
HOUSTON, TEXAS

JESUS IS THE MEDIATOR

1 Timothy 2:1-5

1 I exhort therefore, that, first of all, supplications, prayers, intercessions, and giving of thanks, be made for all men;
2 For kings, and for all that are in authority; that we may lead a quiet and peaceable life in all godliness and honesty.
3 For this is good and acceptable in the sight of God our Saviour;
4 Who will have all men to be saved, and to come unto the knowledge of the truth.
5 For there is one God, and one mediator between God and men, the man Christ Jesus

THE GREAT HYMN
I MUST TELL JESUS

I must tell Jesus
All of my trials
I cannot bear these burdens alone
In my distress
He kindly will help me
He ever cares and loves His own

I must tell Jesus
All of my troubles
He's a kind and compassionate friend
If I but ask Him
He will deliver
Make of my troubles
Quickly an end

I must tell Jesus
I must tell Jesus
I cannot bear these burdens alone
I must tell Jesus, I must tell Jesus
Jesus can help me, Jesus alone

Tempted and tried I need a great savior
One who can help my burdens to bear
I must tell Jesus, I must tell Jesus
He all my cares and sorrows will share

I must tell Jesus
I must tell Jesus
I cannot bear these burdens alone
I must tell Jesus, I must tell Jesus
Jesus can help me, Jesus alone

Unto thee, O God, do I place my trust. Thankfully and joyfully, I have come into Your presence. My spirit is overwhelmed with thoughts of Your grace. My mind spends restless moments going to and fro as I grapple within the finite boundaries of my human reasoning to comprehend the depth of Your love for me. God, I realize that You are too transcendent for me to understand, but my soul rejoices to know that in the distance between my current condition and Your throne stands a mediator who speaks my language. And thank You, Jesus, for all that You are to me—for it is in Your authority that I pray. Amen.

Article 4

**THE GREAT HIM
JESUS IS THE MEDIATOR
1 Timothy 2:1-5**

by
Dr. Kenneth G. Campbell

I believe in justice, but I am a bigger fan of grace. Justice is concerned with what's fair and right. Grace simply gives, even when the recipient is undeserving. God is owed a debt, payable in measurements prescribed through justice, judgment, and wrath because of our sin. As sinners, we cannot pay the balance and are therefore left bankrupt, unforgiven, unclean, and disqualified from our relationship with the Father. But, thank God for grace!

In April 1992, Hall of Fame football legend Jim Brown convened a group of young men in a Watts housing project and worked out a treaty to stop the violence and killings that were going on in Los Angeles, California, in the wake of the Rodney King acquittals. He bravely stood between formerly hostile Bloods and Crips and encouraged the young men to put their guns down and pick up pens to ink the deal. A similar scene took place in March 2019, at the death of Rapper Nipsey Hussle. Compton's adversaries signed a truce to honor his death and what he stood for in life. In life and death, both men became arbiters of peace and saved an incalculable number of lives. In the spiritual sense, a much greater type of mediatory skill is required to bring reconciliation between God's vision and the vices of man.

Sin was originally presented to humankind in the Garden of Eden. It hovered in the backdrop of the Creation story as a dangerous option to be declined and resisted if the first humans were to maintain union with the founder of every inch of the universe. Scripture records the fateful tragedy, wherein God's beloved creation blatantly rebelled against their Creator (see Genesis 2–3). Adam and Eve succumbed to Satan's enticements and betrayed the admonitions of the Father. Their fateful decision that day has plagued humanity ever since. The following results were a forfeiture of paradise and a life disconnected from their Lord. Every decision that goes contrary to the Word of the Lord sets us up for a "fall" and puts us in opposition, or at enmity, with the very One who gives us life (see Romans 8:7).

God and man were now at odds, a far cry from the relationship's original vision that began in the Father's own heart. Their disconnect reached its pinnacle in a grievous separation. Divinity and humanity were "divorced" for the first time due to irreconcilable differences. There seemed to be no reasonable path toward a reunion. The dispute centered around a seemingly insurmountable dilemma. On the one hand, you've got a loving, yet absolutely, Holy God—and on the other is sinful humankind, so desperately in need of the love and grace only found in the Lord of glory.

Each are uniquely hindered from closing the gulf, separating them from one another. God is too holy or "other than" to traverse humanity's sinfulness to procure his redemption. In contrast, man is too sinful to enter God's holiness, in which lies his opportunity to be cleansed. So, there existed an uncrossable chasm, an irreparable breach.

Although both parties possessed the desire to reconcile, they remained alienated by the laws of justice. Our ancestors knew the penalty for partaking of the Tree of the Knowledge of Good and Evil, yet still yielded to its appeal. They were spiritually dead and separated at first bite. Physical death would soon follow. Later, the patriarch Job would lend his voice to humanity's cry, adding to his list of sufferings and despair a desire for a mediator, or "go-between" (see Job 9:33).

In Christ the God-Man rests divinity's (and humanity's) only hopeful possibility. The apparent requirements would be someone who could fairly represent both parties. Scripture teaches that there is only one singular and unique God. and He chooses to manifest Himself in the person of His own son, who is our Mediator (see 1 Timothy 2:5). Professor Richard A. Muller summarizes Reformed and Protestant scholastics regarding Christ's unique role, arguing that "neither nature by itself could mediate between God and man and that both natures, together, perform the opus theandricum, or divine-human work; therefore, Christ is Mediator according to both natures."

Functioning as a prophet, Christ represents the spoken Word of God to which we are to be held accountable. As a priest, He offers, instead becomes, our sacrifice to satisfy the debts we owed to the Judge of the cosmos. In the words of the late John R. W. Stott, He stands "between two worlds," bridging the gap that kept us apart! Jesus' sacrifice on the Cross provided for us unlimited possibilities in life and living. As our Mediator, He intervenes, negotiates, and brokers for us a most excellent covenant with the Father (see Hebrews 8:6). However,

Christ's sacrifice does not end simply on Calvary. He continues to stand between us and our grief, gloom, depression, sorrow, defeat, brokenness, and all other challenges we face in life. As a result of His intervention, we now live victorious in the joyous truth that nothing can separate us from our Lord's eternal love in Jesus Christ (see Romans 8:37-39). Praise Him! The debt is paid. The dispute is settled. How thankful we ought to be, to have a "go-between" for every life experience!

Works Cited

Muller, Richard A. *Dictionary of Latin and Greek Theological Terms*. Grand Rapids: Baker Book House Company, 1985.

Stott, John R. W. *Between Two Worlds*. Grand Rapids: Wm. B. Eerdmans Publishing Company, 1982.

THE GREAT HYMN
I NEED THEE EVERY HOUR

I need thee every hour
Most gracious Lord
No tender voice like thine
Can peace afford
I need thee oh I need thee
Every hour I need thee
Oh bless me now my savior
I come to thee

I need thee every hour
Stay thou near by
Temptations loose their power
When thou art nigh
I need thee oh I need thee
Every hour I need thee
Oh bless me now my savior
I come to thee

I need thee every hour
Most holy one
Oh make me thine indeed
Thou blessed son
I need thee oh I need thee
Every hour I need thee
Oh bless me now my savior
I come to thee
Oh I need thee
I need thee
Oh bless me now my savior
I come to thee

DR. BRYAN L. CARTER
Concord Church
Dallas, Texas

DR. BRYAN L. CARTER
CONCORD CHURCH
DALLAS, TEXAS

JESUS IS THE MASTER

Mark 4:35-38

35 And the same day, when the even was come, he saith unto them, Let us pass over unto the other side.

36 And when they had sent away the multitude, they took him even as he was in the ship. And there were also with him other little ships.

37 And there arose a great storm of wind, and the waves beat into the ship, so that it was now full.

38 And he was in the hinder part of the ship, asleep on a pillow: and they awake him, and say unto him, Master, carest thou not that we perish?

THE GREAT HYMN
MASTER THE TEMPEST IS RAGING

Master, the tempest is raging
Oh, the billows are tossing high
The sky is o'ershadowed with blackness
Oh, no shelter or help is nigh
Carest thou not that we perish?
How canst we lie, how canst thou lie asleep
Asleep when each moment so madly is threatning
A grave, a grave, a grave in the angry deep?
Get up, Jesus, because
The winds and the waves shall obey thy will

All you got to say is
Peace, be still
Peace, be still
Peace, be still
Peace, be still

Whether the wrath of the storm-tossed sea
Or demons, or men, or whatever it be
No water can swallow the ship where lies
The master of ocean and earth and sky...

Eternal Master, God of glory, friend of sinners and teacher of every disciple, my soul looks up to Thee as the only sacrifice of Calvary needed to wash my sins away. Your spotless life will forever be a light to me as I strive in time to become more like You. Master, teach me every day Your way, guide each moment in Your mercy, and order my steps in such a way that I never go astray but that I live each moment in humble obedience to Your will for the life that You have granted me to live. In the name of Jesus Christ I pray. Amen!

Article 5

**THE GREAT HIM
JESUS IS THE MASTER**
Mark 4:35-38

by
Dr. Bryan L. Carter

Storms Come

Mark 4:35-41 opens with this reality that storms come. The disciples were in the boat with Jesus and a storm came out of nowhere! It was a total surprise, for they knew better than to travel when storms were anticipated. But on this occasion, the weather report was positive before it dramatically changed. The Sea of Galilee had a reputation for fierce storms because the climate favored storms. The Sea of Galilee rests at 628 feet below sea level and is surrounded by the Mt. Hermon mountain range, reaching 9,200 feet above sea level and gouged with deep ravines. These ravines serve as gigantic funnels to focus whirling winds down onto the lake without notice. The cold air from the mountains encounters the warm air from the lake, and you immediately have the perfect environment for storms. These storms can be so ferocious that they can cause a boat to sink.

In 1986, the hull of a fishing boat was recovered from the mud on the northwest shore of the Sea of Galilee, about five miles south of Capernaum. The ship—26½ feet long, 7½ feet wide, and 4½ feet high—corresponds in design to the first-century mosaic of a Galilean boat preserved in Migdal only a mile from the discovery site. The boat was propelled by four rowers (two per side) and has a total capacity of about fifteen persons.

A boat like this one is probably the kind of vessel they utilized in that day. Although their storm was physical, we know what it is like to face all types of storms ourselves. For example, there can be health storms, marriage storms, parenting storms, emotional storms, relationships storms, career storms, financial storms, family storms, or mental storms. We know what it is like when your boat is filling up and the pressure and difficulty it can bring. These were not inexperienced sailors; these were experienced sailors, yet they still knew that they were in over their heads. They saw the horrible conditions and began to use their training and experience to work their way out of the storm—but eventually, their training and experience were not enough. They tried to rescue themselves. We too know what it's like to try to rescue ourselves from storms. We have all tried to figure our way out, plan our way out, or manipulate our way out.

Storms Cause

Storms can cause many things in our lives. They can cause us to take inventory of our lives. When the disciples realized that they could not do this independently, they began to enlist and call for anyone on the boat. They called for Peter, called for Matthew, called for Thomas, and probably called every name they could imagine. Finally, someone realized that they needed to get Jesus; Jesus was still asleep at the bottom of the boat. Jesus had slept through the entire storm. The ship was rocking and swaying, and water was coming in, yet He was still sleeping. All the chaos and calamity were going on around Him, yet He still slept. Everybody else was worried and panicking, but Jesus was sleeping the time away. What a picture—that amid the storm, He was sleeping it away. His sleeping is meant to be in contrast to the disciples' panic. He sleeps, and they panic. Ironically, the only time in the Gospels that we hear of Jesus sleeping is during a storm.

Finally, somebody decided to wake up Jesus. I believe they were shocked that He was still sleeping, but they knew that when they woke Him up, He would know what to do. So, they grabbed Him by the shoulder or pushed him, and He woke up. I believe they woke Him up by faith. They didn't know what He would do, but I believe they woke Him up because they trusted that He would do *something*. They had been with Jesus long enough to trust that He could do something about it.

Storms cause us to ask questions: "Teacher, don't you care if we drown?" The disciples felt as though at the time they needed Him most, Jesus was asleep. They were disappointed with his apparent inactivity. Have you ever had a time in your life when the apparent inactivity of Jesus made you believe that He didn't care? It is a common experience for us to feel in our storms that Jesus doesn't care.

- If He cared, I wouldn't have lost my job.
- If He cared, I wouldn't be struggling like I am now.
- If He cared, I wouldn't have gotten sick.

If we are honest, there are times in life when it seems that Jesus has forgotten about us and left us all by ourselves. The storm became a teaching tool. Storms are part of the growing process. God will allow you to go through the storm to teach you something about Him. Storms cause us to learn new lessons.

Storms will teach you who your real friends are. Storms will teach you how to pray. Storms will teach you how to be humble. Storms will teach you on whom you can depend. Although the storm surprised them, it didn't surprise Him. God sees every wave; He knows your heart rate, respiration, thoughts, emotions, dreams, and everything.

Storms Cease

Jesus got up and spoke to the waves. He speaks to inanimate objects. This is called anthropomorphism in theology. He rebukes the wind and tells it to be quiet. He talks to the wind like we speak to the TV during our favorite movie. When Jesus speaks, something happens. Something happens because they recognize His voice. Even nature has to come to attention because His voice is the voice that created the heavens and the earth. His voice brought healing to a sick girl, mobility to a lame man, and sight to a blind man.

His word can work in your life as well if you stand on His Word. There is an immediate result of His speaking. There is total transformation achieved by Jesus' intervention. There is a supernatural change in the weather because of His words. Jesus' power over the forces of nature, and the language in which it is described, foreshadows His power over the forces that disrupt human nature in the story of the Gerasene demoniac (see Mark 5:1-20).

Throughout the stilling of the storm, Mark gives clues that the miracle's purpose is for the disciples. The story is told from their perspective: it is they who take Jesus with them (see 4:36) and raise Him from sleep (4:38); they are afraid (4:41), and their probing question concludes the story (4:41). This is an unusual perspective for Mark, who is typically an anonymous narrator. In addition, the narrative focus of the story is on faith.

Jesus asked His disciples, "Why are you so afraid? Do you still have no faith?" He does not criticize their knowledge that they did know enough but did not have faith to trust Him regardless of the circumstances. They were unable to respond with confidence in a crisis. The response of Jesus overwhelmed them. That's just like Jesus to leave you speechless and overwhelmed in His response.

Conclusion

Our response to this passage is to have faith in Jesus; always remember that there are no circumstances, situations, or persons that He cannot handle; Jesus is master of all!

THE GREAT HYMN
LIKE A SHIP THAT'S TOSSED AND DRIVEN

Like a ship that's tossed and driven
Battered by an angry sea
When the storms of life are raging
And their fury falls on me
I wonder what I have done
That makes this race so hard to run
Then I say to my soul, take courage
The Lord will make a way somehow
The Lord will make a way somehow
When beneath the stars I bow
He will take away each sorrow
There will be no sad tomorrow
Many a nights I toss in pain
Wondering what the day might be bringing
Then I say to my soul, take your courage
The Lord will make a way somehow

Many a nights I tossed and turn
Wondering what the day might bring
Then I say to my soul, take your courage
The Lord will make a way somehow
The Lord will make a way somehow
When beneath the stars I bow
He will take away each sorrow
There will be no sad tomorrow

DR. TELLIS J. CHAPMAN
Galilee Missionary Baptist Church
Detroit, Michigan

Dr. Tellis J. Chapman
Galilee Missionary Baptist Church
Detroit, Michigan

JESUS IS THE LAMB OF GOD

John 1:19-29

19 And this is the record of John, when the Jews sent priests and Levites from Jerusalem to ask him, Who art thou?

20 And he confessed, and denied not; but confessed, I am not the Christ.

21 And they asked him, What then? Art thou Elias? And he saith, I am not. Art thou that prophet? And he answered, No.

22 Then said they unto him, Who art thou? that we may give an answer to them that sent us. What sayest thou of thyself?

23 He said, I am the voice of one crying in the wilderness, Make straight the way of the Lord, as said the prophet Esaias.

24 And they which were sent were of the Pharisees.

25 And they asked him, and said unto him, Why baptizest thou then, if thou be not that Christ, nor Elias, neither that prophet?

26 John answered them, saying, I baptize with water: but there standeth one among you, whom ye know not;

27 He it is, who coming after me is preferred before me, whose shoe's latchet I am not worthy to unloose.

28 These things were done in Bethabara beyond Jordan, where John was baptizing.

29 The next day John seeth Jesus coming unto him, and saith, Behold the Lamb of God, which taketh away the sin of the world.

THE GREAT HYMN
THE BLOOD

The blood that Jesus shed for me
Way back on Calvary
The blood that gives me strength
From day to day
It will never lose its power

It reaches to the highest mountain
It flows to the lowest valley
The blood that gives me strength
From day to day
It will never lose its power

It soothes my doubts and calms my fears
And it dries all my tears
The blood that gives me strength
From day to day
It will never lose its power

It reaches to the highest mountain
It flows to the lowest valley
The blood that gives me strength
From day to day
It will never lose its power

Everlasting Father and God of all glory, I approach You this very moment with a reverent degree of fear. When I consider my human flaws, my personal inadequacies, my private hang-ups, and my apparent sins, my soul shouts "woe is me" every time I think about coming near You. However, intertwined in my fear is a Lamb—a sacrifice that is so perfect that its blood would cleanse me forever. As I bow my head and whisper this prayer, my soul shouts and dances. My heart screams with gracious vitality before You even now; I thank Jesus for being my crucified Lamb. I have but one petition to lay before You at present and that is this: cause me to live in such a way that when others come to know me, they meet and love the Lamb that saved me. In Jesus' name I pray. Amen.

Article 6

THE GREAT HIM
JESUS IS THE LAMB OF GOD
John 1:19-29

"HERE HE IS"

by
Dr. Tellis J. Chapman

Whatever condition the world is in, there's still a possibility for the world to be converted. Have you taken a look at the world lately? Have you noticed it is horrifying, horrendous, sickening, sinister, and in a sordid status and state of affairs? It seems that there is always a scandal, and greed-stricken people are in pursuit of a personal empire. It has come to be a quest for power at any cost and a tolerance for corruption. It has come to hell-oriented environments; hatred and high crime rates; murder; and uncontrollable madness. It has come to incest, injustice, intolerance, indignity, and anger. It has come to jail and prison population overflow; stressful jobs and hostile work environments; bitter race relations and disconcerted religion; marginalization and disenfranchisement; gentrification; suicide; genocide; senseless homicides; and corrupt leadership in government. It has come to pedophile pastors; pimping preachers and prostituting churches; reality shows for entertainment; adolescent mothers and pregnant prom queens; deadbeat dads and dysfunctional homes; tainted talk shows and adulterated TV; carefree actors and foul-mouthed rap artists; hideous and horrendous human trafficking; lawless, law-breaking lawmakers; classism; sexism; xenophobia; and homophobia. It has come to romanticized, commodified, and commercialized Easter and Christmas seasons. It has come to be a very noticeable "divided states of America," prompted by "Trumpsters" who forever want to "make America great again." The world, therefore, needs rescuing from itself. But rescue is only possible with God. Despite the conditions to which the world has come, it becomes an inspiration for all of us to take a look at who has come to the world! John called Him the "Lamb of God."

There is speculation as to who this John was. However, it is without question that he was a Jewish author, a Palestinian, and an eyewitness of Jesus (see John 1:14). Unfortunately, the book nowhere tells us who this disciple was. Evidence shows that the most probable identification is with the apostle John. Even though the authorship is deliberated, the writer's objective is to communicate Jesus as God (see John 1:1-14). Moreover, for salvific riposte to those whose dialogical exchanges are overloaded with interrogatives about the solution for humanity's worst hang-up, there is a resounding response from the annals of biblical history: Here He is!

History has always presented prominent personalities, contributors to the well-being of society. They were liberators of slavery and oppression; culture-shaping pontificators; drumbeats for justice; and color-barrier breakers in the White House—all of whom provoked our ethos and redirected history. But Jesus Christ is the only one who personifies the profile of the one qualified to reconcile the abysmal breach between God and humanity. John, while performing a ritualistic baptism unto repentance for penitent sinners, announced Jesus' portrayal as the Lamb of God. Wiersbe considered this statement to be a summation of God's Word. In one sense, the message of the Bible can be summed up in this title. The question in the Old Testament is, "Where is the lamb?" (Genesis 22:7b). In the four Gospels, the emphasis is "Behold the Lamb of God!" This is an awe-inspiring announcement, as it established the compassion of God that bequeathed helpless humanity with a solution worthy of intense scrutiny.

This announcement distinguishes a Person of Particular Personage. Of all the outstanding personalities that have been on the proverbial world stage, Jesus, by far, is the most intriguing, curative, salutatory figure in history. He is the only person whose birth changes the calculation of history from BC to AD. He personifies the maxim for human behavior and is the infallible template of holy exactness. John employed a definite article when announcing the arrival of Jesus on the baptismal scene by saying, "the Lamb of God," *Ho amnos toú Theoú*, meaning the lamb that has been provided by God. Moreover, He is *the* Lamb, not *a* lamb. He is the "loaf and the leaven" for salvific consumption, a characteristic that distinguishes Him from common contributors of ordinary creation.

This announcement discloses an Individual of Unprecedented Mercy. We live in a cold, calloused, indifferent, and incredulous society, one that calls for a person with a benevolent spirit for rescue—not a spirit that bares outlandish exigencies but, rather, one that is sensitive to a conscience-stricken penitent sinner realizing that he or she is a candidate for redemption. This will never come from anti-democratic mercenaries, inhumane tyrants, or sadistic political figures. Nor will it ever be a part of the résumé of people of parsimonious personality. This is an expression of mercy that can only come from one who encountered sin ἁμαρτία *hamartia*, meaning "to miss the true end and scope of our lives, which is God." Moreover, Jesus encountered sin but never became a sinner. Jesus Christ gave a human face to mercy and marched up blood-stained altar steps and was sacrificed for sinners, irrespective of race, social class, creed, color, or personal sin-laced antiquity. Moreover, His mercy suited our case. He came to take away our sins, exonerate our guilty status, and reconcile our ruptured relationship with God.

Lastly, this announcement denotes an All-Inclusive Agenda. Jesus Christ is not biased with His blessings, nor is He fastidious with His favors. His salvific schema bespeaks a calculated undertaking that incorporated the whole world. His omniscience contemplated every aspect of human vicissitude, ruminated every trespass, and still counted us in. John recognized Jesus beyond His "Jew-ness" and stipulated the integration of Gentiles. This agenda would eventuate into a misinterpreted storyline for the impervious religious sect of Jews who wanted Jesus to make Jerusalem "great again." They perceived the Messiah to be one who would interdict Herod's influence, overthrow Roman rule, unseat Emperor Caesar, instigate political recovery, and reestablish the throne of the late King David. Moreover, He came and stood at the behest of the inheritors of eternal doom and responded as the sole benefactor for the "whosoever crowd." John declared, "He is the Lamb of God who takes away the sin of the world."

To conclude the matter, for all interrogatives relative to Christ's presence and purpose historically and existentially—for those who are forever depressed, dejected, hurt, heartbroken, marginalized, oppressed, lost, and without love in this unconverted world—listen to the loquacious verbiage of John during an awakening baptism ceremony. Here He is!

THE GREAT HYMN
THE OLD RUGGED CROSS

On a hill far away stood an old rugged cross
The emblem of suffering and shame
And I love that old cross where the dearest and best
For a world of lost sinners was slain

So I'll cherish the old rugged cross
Till my trophies at last I lay down
And I will cling to the old rugged cross
And exchange it some day for a crown

To the old rugged cross I will ever be true
It's shame and reproach gladly bear
Then he'll call me someday to my home far away
Where his glory forever I'll share

And I'll cherish the old rugged cross
Till my trophies at last I lay down
And I will cling to the old rugged cross
And exchange it some day for a crown
I will cling to the old rugged cross
And exchange it some day for a crown

DR. MARCUS D. COSBY
Wheeler Avenue Baptist Church
Houston, Texas

DR. MARCUS D. COSBY
WHEELER AVENUE BAPTIST CHURCH
HOUSTON, TEXAS

JESUS IS OUR HOPE

1 Timothy 1:1-7

1 Paul, an apostle of Jesus Christ by the commandment of God our Saviour, and Lord Jesus Christ, which is our hope;

2 Unto Timothy, my own son in the faith: Grace, mercy, and peace, from God our Father and Jesus Christ our Lord.

3 As I besought thee to abide still at Ephesus, when I went into Macedonia, that thou mightest charge some that they teach no other doctrine,

4 Neither give heed to fables and endless genealogies, which minister questions, rather than godly edifying which is in faith: so do.

5 Now the end of the commandment is charity out of a pure heart, and of a good conscience, and of faith unfeigned:

6 From which some having swerved have turned aside unto vain jangling;

7 Desiring to be teachers of the law; understanding neither what they say, nor whereof they affirm.

THE GREAT HYMN
ON CHRIST THE SOLID ROCK I STAND

My hope is built on nothing less
Than Jesus' blood and righteousness

I dare not trust the sweetest frame
But wholly lean on Jesus' name
On Christ the solid rock I stand
All other ground is sinking sand
All other ground is sinking sand

When darkness veils his lovely face
I rest on His unchanging grace
In every high and stormy gale
My anchor holds within the veil
His oath, his covenant, his blood
Supports me in the 'whelming flood

When all around my soul gives way
He then is all my hope and stay
On Christ the solid rock I stand
All other ground is sinking sand
All other ground is sinking sand

When He shall come with trumpet sound
Oh may I then in Him be found
Dressed in his righteousness alone
Faultless to stand before the throne

On Christ the solid rock I stand
All other ground is sinking sand
All other ground is sinking sand
On Christ the solid rock I stand
All other ground is sinking sand
All other ground is sinking sand

Loving, kind, and merciful Master, thank You for allowing me this moment of prayerful consideration at Your throne. I praise, honor, and bless You because You alone are the creator of the cosmos, the architect of the universe, and the engineer of all creation. O Lord, I revere You, fear You, adore You, appreciate You, and seek to satisfy You each moment You allow me to live. Yet, O God, when I canvas the landscape of my ever-present reality, there are times when a cloud of hopeless despair seems to find me. God, when I consider global poverty, famine, and infirmity, when I look at disease, disheartened countries, and oppressed people the whole world over, my soul weeps. But, my tears do not last long. I know in the bowels and mercies of my soul that things will not always be like this, because You are my hope—a hope that stretches from everlasting to everlasting! In Jesus' name I pray. Amen.

Article 7

**THE GREAT HIM
JESUS IS OUR HOPE**
1 Timothy 1:1-7

by
Dr. Marcus D. Cosby

Indeed, it is possible to have a discussion regarding Jesus Christ as our hope without its mention, but the Christian Church has so benefitted from the seminal work of Edward Mote and William Bradbury, who set to music that classic hymn "The Solid Rock," that it just begs to be included at the outset of this presentation—for its lyrics make clear that our Christian reality is rooted in the fact that the Lord Jesus has secured for us so great a salvation through His blood at Calvary and His righteousness throughout His life and ministry. As a consequence of that strong and secure foundation, we are able to build our hope on such a reality.

Elpis, the Greek word from which we get our English word *hope*, speaks to the desire for some good with the expectation of obtaining it. When Paul writes to his protégé in the faith, he does so to ensure that false doctrine does not permeate the minds of the people of the Church in Ephesus, where Timothy gives leadership in Paul's absence. To mention that Jesus is our hope further emphasizes the reality that He is the Solid Rock on which the Church must stand in an effort to withstand the forceful winds of heretical teaching that seek to overcome God's people.

In a world still filled with heresy and hopelessness, we must be reminded of the good that comes through the life and liberty of Jesus Christ, who ensures that we always have an expectation beyond that which we can see. To be sure, racial unrest, social injustice, and the abundance of suffering and other ills that plague our world often cause us to say, like the remnant of the House of Israel in that Mesopotamian Valley of Dry Bones, "our hope is lost" (Ezekiel 37:11). It is this very mentality that led the Johnson brothers to pen the timeless Negro national anthem, "Lift Every Voice and Sing," whose second stanza affirms, "Stony the road we trod, bitter the chastening rod, Felt in the days when hope unborn had died . . . ."

Void a relationship with Jesus, even the Church may be duped into believing that our unborn hope has already died. As Black people are gunned down in the streets of our cities by those who are paid to protect and serve, some in our congregations pitiably say, "Our hope is gone!" As our political landscape is continually peppered with idiocy and contemptibility, the voices of progressive citizens are raised all the more: "Our hope is gone!" As the health of the nations is threatened by a pandemic that does not discriminate on the basis of any reality, many who no longer have any expectation remaining sorrowfully exclaim, "Our hope is gone!" So, Paul emphatically reminds Timothy and all of the Lord's people that Jesus is our hope! He is the one who guarantees that the good we desire is fulfilled as we faithfully maintain our expectations of Him.

Perhaps the Apostle makes this powerful declaration to encourage Timothy amid that false doctrine. It is evident in Paul's second letter to Timothy that his mentee could be given to timidity. The reverberating remarks of 2 Timothy 1:6-7 make clear that Timothy was to "stir up the gift of God [within him, remembering that] God hath not given us the spirit of fear; but of power, and of love, and of a sound mind." We often close the citation with the recitation of verse 7, but I suggest that verse 8 continues Paul's pastoral advice to be emboldened through our hope, who is Jesus. Paul says, "Do not be ashamed of the testimony about our Lord or of me, His prisoner. Rather, join with me in suffering for the gospel, by the power of God" (emphasis and paraphrase mine).

Please permit me to suggest further that our hope, who is Jesus, enlightens us amid the dreariness of the aforementioned existential realities to which we are exposed. Without Jesus, we are left to meander through the murky maze of life without any light at the end of our proverbial tunnels. So, when Paul speaks to the Church at Colosse, he exhorts them to be steadfast despite their sufferings—because they have Christ in them, and He is our hope of glory (see Colossians 1:27). The Greek word *Doxa* can be variously defined as "reputation, appearance, brilliance; to think and thereby recognize a person or thing for who or what it really is." The definition that stands out for our purposes here is "brilliance"; it provides the effect of illumination or brightness that is found in Jesus Christ. As I write this, I can hear the Saints at Emmanuel Baptist Church in Chicago, the church of my Christian development, raising their voices every December to sing, "We'll walk in the light, beautiful light, come where the dewdrops of mercy are bright, shine all around us by day and by night, Jesus, the Light of the world!" With darkness comes despair, which robs us of our expectation. Therefore, we need Jesus to enlighten our experiences with the hope that only He can provide. He is the hope of glory. His brilliant reputation will be revealed despite the current context in which we find ourselves—however dismal, depressing, demoralizing, or distressing that context may appear.

Surely, it is possible to discuss Jesus Christ as our hope without the mention of that great church hymn. Still, even as Timothy heard the voice of his mentor while reading his missive, I mysteriously hear the voice of my mentor and faithful father in the ministry, Dr. L. K. Curry, closing his Sunday sermon rejoicing in the reality that *on Christ, the solid Rock, I stand—all other ground is sinking sand, all other ground is sinking sand.* Dear friend, we can have great expectations that we will obtain some good in this world (that is filled with so much worse) because Jesus is our hope! To Him be the glory, both now and forever, AMEN.

THE GREAT HYMN
O HOW I LOVE JESUS

There is a name I love to hear
I love to sing its worth
It sounds like music in my ear
The sweetest name on earth
Oh, how I love Jesus
Oh, how I love Jesus
Oh, how I love Jesus
Because He first loved me

It tells me of a Savior's love
Who died and set me free
It tells me of His precious blood
The sinner's perfect plea
Oh, how I love Jesus
Oh, how I love Jesus
Oh, how I love Jesus
Because He first loved me

It tells of One whose loving heart
Can feel my deepest woe
Who in each sorrow bears a part
That none can bear below
Oh, how I love Jesus
Oh, how I love Jesus
Oh, how I love Jesus
Because He first loved me

Oh, how I love Jesus
Oh, how I love Jesus
Oh, how I love Jesus
Because He first loved me

REVEREND MARISSA R. FARROW
Greater Allen A.M.E. Cathedral
Queens, New York

REVEREND MARISSA R. FARROW
GREATER ALLEN A.M.E. CATHEDRAL
QUEENS, NEW YORK

JESUS IS OUR FRIEND

John 15:9-17 (focus on verse 15)

9 As the Father hath loved me, so have I loved you: continue ye in my love.

10 If ye keep my commandments, ye shall abide in my love; even as I have kept my Father's commandments, and abide in his love.

11 These things have I spoken unto you, that my joy might remain in you, and that your joy might be full.

12 This is my commandment, That ye love one another, as I have loved you.

13 Greater love hath no man than this, that a man lay down his life for his friends.

14 Ye are my friends, if ye do whatsoever I command you.

15 Henceforth I call you not servants; for the servant knoweth not what his lord doeth: but I have called you friends; for all things that I have heard of my Father I have made known unto you.

16 Ye have not chosen me, but I have chosen you, and ordained you, that ye should go and bring forth fruit, and that your fruit should remain: that whatsoever ye shall ask of the Father in my name, he may give it you.

17 These things I command you, that ye love one another.

THE GREAT HYMN
WHAT A FRIEND WE HAVE IN JESUS

What a friend we have in Jesus
All our sins and griefs to bear
And what a privilege to carry
Everything to God in prayer
Oh, what peace we often forfeit
Oh, what needless pain we bear
All because we do not carry
Everything to God in prayer

Have we trials and temptations?
Is there trouble anywhere?
We should never be discouraged
Take it to the Lord in prayer
Can we find a friend so faithful
Who will all our sorrows share?
Jesus knows our every weakness
Take it to the Lord in prayer

There are times, Lord, when I feel lonely. It is as if no one understands. In those silent, dark moments, O God, I feel abandoned and lonely. But You, O Lord, have always been the lifter of my bowed-down head. You have forever been my light in times of darkness. You have been the keeper of my secrets, the forgiver of my sins, the lover of my soul, and my strength in times of weakness. Thank You, Lord, for being my friend; having You as my friend makes life worth living every day. In the name of Jesus I pray. Amen.

Article 8

THE GREAT HIM
JESUS IS OUR FRIEND
John 15:9-17

"MEMBERSHIP HAS ITS PRIVILEGES"

by
Reverend Marissa R. Farrow

As with any relationship in which we engage ourselves, some expectations come with an association that we can only have because of connection. A relationship is like a qualifier in many senses, in that it allows you insight and engagement that strangers cannot receive. There's an exclusivity to a relationship, like a company that gives more value and benefits to their loyal consumers. It's the blessing and covering of a relationship.

I recently was driving home from New York City, and I was just about 35 minutes away from my home at about 1:00 a.m. when I discovered that my passenger-side tire had gone flat—fast. As I pulled over, I discovered that there was a piece of metal in my tire that was too large for me to have plugged or to change. After trying to avoid the necessity of lengthiness, I knew it would come if I had to wait for someone to help me. I picked up my phone and couldn't think of where to begin—because I knew I had allowed my AAA roadside membership to be canceled. Along with it went the benefit of calling and knowing that I could immediately receive help that would cost me a fraction of what I would have to pay were I not a member.

There are some things you simply will not be able to access without a relationship. There are some doors you may not be permitted to walk through and some blessings and opportunities in which you won't be able to partake without a solidified association that says *I belong to God, and He, in turn, belongs to me.* That's what we see personified in John 15:15, where Jesus shares in this message to us that He doesn't consider us unworthy of the benefits of knowing Christ—but that He identifies us as worthy of knowing, worthy of the insight that we can gain by being connected. Jesus says this: *I don't minimize you down to servants, as they do not know the business of the master. But I call you friends, because I share My knowledge even with you.*

Jesus tells us, *Everything that I learned from My Father I have made known to you*. He leaves it in the word, with the prophets, with the writers. He's even given it to us in signs and divine interventions and revelations. We have the key to an understanding of being in partnership with Christ. He shares with us the knowledge that He shares about God and His heart, will, and desires for us. That's why I love the words of the old church hymn that echo 'til this day, "What a friend we have in Jesus, all of our sins and griefs to bear; what a privilege to carry, everything to God in prayer." The words join in the confirmation of truth found in the Word: that when you have a friend like Jesus, someone you can talk to, look to, and lean and depend on, He, like a friend, will respond with encouragement. That is often found in the Word of God. But it leads us to the truth that Jesus can extend to us—even through the message of His life and victory of the Cross—the plans, thoughts, and heart of God for us. Sometimes we stand in need of a gentle reminder that God's plans for us will always lead us to victory, even when we cannot see past the grueling process that it often takes to get to that victory. When we talk to Jesus and cast our cares upon Him, He can share His knowledge and even experience about God, His and our Father. To remind us that His ways may not be our ways nor His thoughts our thoughts, but He still loves and cares for us despite the things we experience in life.

It is so easy to become overwhelmed when life is against you. But it's a different thing when you have the assurance of knowing that you are friends with Christ, who has shared in our experience and who understands what it is to wonder sometimes where your father is in the midst of bad seasons. Jesus says, *I don't see you as a servant but as a friend*. One is worthy of the blessing bestowed upon him or her who shares a connection. Remember that Christ is not standing by but standing with us, prepared to share with us the heart of God that can only come from having a relationship with Him.

This is why I always exercise extreme gratitude to be a friend of our Savior; it is the relationship that we must value most in our lives because it is that insight that will help us make it through our lives. There are some things I know about the Father—from the things I have witnessed Him do through His Son and things the Son knows about the Father that He shares with us. If you are reading this and you are unsure of the status of your relationship with Jesus Christ, take it from me: there's no greater blessing one can have than to be called a friend of Christ's.

THE GREAT HYMN
THERE'S NOT A FRIEND LIKE THE LOWLY JESUS

There's not a friend like the lowly Jesus,
No, not one! No, not one!
None else could heal all our soul's diseases,
No, not one! No, not one!

Jesus knows all about our struggles,
He will guide till the day is done;
There's not a friend like the lowly Jesus,
No, not one! No, not one!

There's not an hour that He is not near us,
No, not one! No, not one!
No night so dark but His love can cheer us,
No, not one! No, not one!

Did ever saint find this Friend forsake him?
No, not one! No, not one!
Or sinner find that He would not take him?
No, not one! No, not one!

Was ever a gift like the Savior given?
No, not one! No, not one!
Will He refuse us a home in Heaven?
No, not one! No, not one!

Just as I am, without one plea
But that Thy blood was shed for me
And that Thou bid'st me come to Thee
O Lamb of God, I come! I come

Just as I am, though tossed about
With many a conflict, many a doubt
Fighting and fears within without
O Lamb of God, I come, I come

PASTOR CHRISTOPHER F. HARTWELL
Crossroads Community Church
Pearland, Texas

PASTOR CHRISTOPHER F. HARTWELL
CROSSROADS COMMUNITY CHURCH
PEARLAND, TEXAS

JESUS IS OUR REDEEMER

Job 19:1-25

1 Then Job answered and said,

2 How long will ye vex my soul, and break me in pieces with words?

3 These ten times have ye reproached me: ye are not ashamed that ye make yourselves strange to me.

4 And be it indeed that I have erred, mine error remaineth with myself.

5 If indeed ye will magnify yourselves against me, and plead against me my reproach:

6 Know now that God hath overthrown me, and hath compassed me with his net.

7 Behold, I cry out of wrong, but I am not heard: I cry aloud, but there is no judgment.

8 He hath fenced up my way that I cannot pass, and he hath set darkness in my paths.

9 He hath stripped me of my glory, and taken the crown from my head.

10 He hath destroyed me on every side, and I am gone: and mine hope hath he removed like a tree.

11 He hath also kindled his wrath against me, and he counteth me unto him as one of his enemies.

12 His troops come together, and raise up their way against me, and encamp round about my tabernacle.

13 He hath put my brethren far from me, and mine acquaintance are verily estranged from me.

14 My kinsfolk have failed, and my familiar friends have forgotten me.

15 They that dwell in mine house, and my maids, count me for a stranger: I am an alien in their sight.

16 I called my servant, and he gave me no answer; I intreated him with my mouth.

17 My breath is strange to my wife, though I intreated for the children's sake of mine own body.

18 Yea, young children despised me; I arose, and they spake against me.

19 All my inward friends abhorred me: and they whom I loved are turned against me.

20 My bone cleaveth to my skin and to my flesh, and I am escaped with the skin of my teeth.

21 Have pity upon me, have pity upon me, O ye my friends; for the hand of God hath touched me.

22 Why do ye persecute me as God, and are not satisfied with my flesh?

23 Oh that my words were now written! oh that they were printed in a book!

24 That they were graven with an iron pen and lead in the rock for ever!

25 For I know that my redeemer liveth, and that he shall stand at the latter day upon the earth.

THE GREAT HYMN
REDEEMED, REDEEMED MY SOUL HAS BEEN REDEEMED

Calvary was the marketplace, where Jesus
purchased my sins,
He struggled up the hill and had no money to give.
An old rugged cross was laid on Him,
He exchanged His life for all my sins;
I've been redeemed by the precious blood of the Lamb.

Although Jesus went to Calvary and
purchased all of my sins,
I still must bear a cross if I ever except to wear a crown.
Had He not redeemed Himself for me,
I would not have life eternally;
I've been redeemed by the precious blood of the Lamb.

I've been redeemed by the precious blood of Jesus,
He paid the price for my sins on Calvary.
He gave His life for me and now I have a right
to the tree of life;
I've been redeemed by the precious blood of the Lamb.

Redeemed, redeemed,
my soul has been redeemed.
Redeemed, redeemed,
my soul has been redeemed.

Washed in the blood,
my soul has been redeemed.
Washed in the blood,
my soul has been redeemed.

Saved, saved,
my soul has been redeemed.
Saved, saved,

Merciful Master, I approach You right now with the Cross on my mind. As I think about Your suffering, sadness, and sorrow that You endured for me that fateful day, I want You to know that my soul is forever indebted to You. Thank You, Lord, for paying a debt that You did not owe because I had a debt that I could not pay. Thank You, O Lord, for becoming sin for me so that I might become a son of Yours. I celebrate You, honor You, and worship You. In the name of Jesus I pray. Amen.

Article 9

THE GREAT HIM
JESUS IS OUR REDEEMER
Job 19:1-25

"HELP IS ON THE WAY"

by
Pastor Christopher F. Hartwell

Suffering is indiscriminate. The mystery of human suffering will not be solved in this lifetime. My attempt in this theological discussion is to examine the unwarranted suffering Job experienced from the hand of a gracious and merciful God. In chapter 19, he makes a declaration that his Redeemer will vindicate him—but how was Job able to say, "I know my Redeemer liveth" after his wife told him to curse God and die and his friends accuse him of things of which he was not guilty?

Of the forty-two chapters that make up the book of Job, chapter 19 is the most familiar and contentious. Chapter 19 is Job's defense to his compassionless comforters' accusations. An examination of Job's entire book provides an understanding that Job ultimately trusted His Redeemer and that the Redeemer trusted Job. Job's experience reminds me of a chorus from Bobby Womack's song entitled, "I Wish He Didn't Trust Me So Much." The assigned text from the book of Job is a work of theodicy according to the Old Testament translator Leo G. Purdue. *Theodicy* can be described as a philosophical discussion of why a good God permits the existence of evil. The truth is that theodicy is a vindication of a good God who allows evil and suffering in the world, making Him appear unjust.

Job is a shadow of what he used to be when he finds himself sitting in ashes, scraping his puss-oozing sores with broken pottery. The evangelist Vance Havner said, "God uses broken things. It takes broken soil to produce a crop, broken clouds to produce rain, broken grain to give bread, broken bread to give strength." God had a conversation that allowed for a permissive power of destruction from Satan on Job's children, cattle, servants, health, and possessions. One can only imagine the pain that Job felt in being considered by God to lose his children, cattle, servants, health, and possessions within a matter of moments. This type of unexpected pain and suffering can be emotionally unbearable to the point where many question God's power and plan for their lives.

Unfortunately, these painful experiences can leave many to feel that they are living under retributive theology. *Retribution theology* is a concept where people feel that God treats them good or bad based on how they behave. Suffering is assumed to be a retributive calamity that comes to those who have done something against the will of God. Therefore, it is believed that when humankind suffers, it is a direct consequence of a sin committed. This idea perpetuated by Satan and communicated to God describes Satan's view of God's relationship with Job, which can be viewed as a modern-day exchange of blessings to reward good behavior. The cause of all this unjustified and undeserved suffering is not apparent. However, this theology of suffering and adversity is where life becomes so problematic that only our Redeemer is able to make sense out of nonsense.

Moreover, Job does not announce to God that His presence is no longer welcome. After all, he had suffered at the hands of Satan; Job sits in ashes, criticized and ridiculed by ten rounds of one-sided judgmental rhetoric from his friends. Job's friends—Eliphaz, Zophar, and Bildad—sit for seven days in silence, practicing social distancing from Job as if what God has considered Job for is contagious. Job's friends hold court and declare that he is guilty until proven innocent. Sound familiar? Particularly when one ponders the current look at the cultural, social, and theological injustices during a global health crisis that has taken the lives of more than two million people worldwide. Black men and women are dying in the custody of those who are deputized to protect and serve; unemployment is on the rise while many people are affected by evictions and foreclosures.

God must have some unknown charges against Job as he sits on the stand in this cosmic courtroom. If God is punishing Job for sin, it was committed unintentionally. *Lord, indict me and set my bail even though I have no money to post my bond.* God had taken the hedge of protection down and walled Job into a net of trials (verse 6). Job says, *I shout for help, but there is no justice* (verse 7). *My friends and family have rejected me while my employees abandon me and treat me like a stranger* (verse 13). *My body is emaciated from sickness and starvation, and my breath is foul because I have no teeth* (verse 17). *Children ridicule me; my former colleagues dislike me because of the disturbing events that God has permitted to happen without cause* (verse 18). If Job died at the corner of persecution and pain, he wanted his epitaph engraved in a book that would outline the unjust, immense suffering he had experienced at the hand of a gracious and merciful God (verses 23-24). Then there is an abrupt shift in Job's language when he makes the declaration, "For I know that my Redeemer lives, and at the last he will stand upon the earth" (verse 25, ESV). The interpretative principle of the passage is that God would stand upon the earth like a witness in the courtroom for the defendant and testify that Job would be innocent.

Job is saying, *I have an obscure knowledge about my Goel* (Hebrew: לגאו; lit. "redeemer"); a *goel* is a person who, as the nearest relative, is charged with the duty of restoring the rights of one who needs relief because of debt, desertion, or death. It is the same way God rescued Israel, and Boaz redeemed Ruth. It is the expectation of death versus the hope of vindication by the hand of his Redeemer—either way, he reasoned, *My help is coming*. Whether it's exoneration in the present or a posthumous redemption, this is the hope the believer has in Christ: that whether we get up or we are caught up, our Redeemer will vindicate us from all unjust suffering that was seemingly without cause.

THE GREAT HYMN
REDEEMER O HOW I LOVE TO PROCLAIM IT

Redeemed, how I love to proclaim it!
Redeemed by the blood of the Lamb;
Redeemed through His infinite mercy,
His child and forever I am.
Refrain

Redeemed, redeemed,
Redeemed by the blood of the Lamb;
Redeemed, redeemed,
His child and forever I am.

Redeemed, and so happy in Jesus,
No language my rapture can tell;
I know that the light of His presence
With me doth continually dwell.

Refrain

I think of my blessèd Redeemer,
I think of Him all the day long:
I sing, for I cannot be silent;
His love is the theme of my song.

Refrain

I know there's a crown that is waiting,
In yonder bright mansion for me,
And soon, with the spirits made perfect,
At home with the Lord I shall be.

DR. FREDERICK D. HAYNES III
Friendship West Baptist Church
Dallas, Texas

DR. FREDERICK D. HAYNES, III
FRIENDSHIP WEST BAPTIST CHURCH
DALLAS, TEXAS

JESUS IS KING OF KINGS

Revelation 17:1-14

1 And there came one of the seven angels which had the seven vials, and talked with me, saying unto me, Come hither; I will shew unto thee the judgment of the great whore that sitteth upon many waters:

2 With whom the kings of the earth have committed fornication, and the inhabitants of the earth have been made drunk with the wine of her fornication.

3 So he carried me away in the spirit into the wilderness: and I saw a woman sit upon a scarlet coloured beast, full of names of blasphemy, having seven heads and ten horns.

4 And the woman was arrayed in purple and scarlet colour, and decked with gold and precious stones and pearls, having a golden cup in her hand full of abominations and filthiness of her fornication:

5 And upon her forehead was a name written, MYSTERY, BABYLON THE GREAT, THE MOTHER OF HARLOTS AND ABOMINATIONS OF THE EARTH.

6 And I saw the woman drunken with the blood of the saints, and with the blood of the martyrs of Jesus: and when I saw her, I wondered with great admiration.

7 And the angel said unto me, Wherefore didst thou marvel? I will tell thee the mystery of the woman, and of the beast that carrieth her, which hath the seven heads and ten horns.

8 The beast that thou sawest was, and is not; and shall ascend out of the bottomless pit, and go into perdition: and they that dwell on the earth shall wonder, whose names were not written in the book of life from the foundation of the world, when they behold the beast that was, and is not, and yet is.

9 And here is the mind which hath wisdom. The seven heads are seven mountains, on which the woman sitteth.

10 And there are seven kings: five are fallen, and one is, and the other is not yet come; and when he cometh, he must continue a short space.

11 And the beast that was, and is not, even he is the eighth, and is of the seven, and goeth into perdition.

12 And the ten horns which thou sawest are ten kings, which have received no kingdom as yet; but receive power as kings one hour with the beast.

13 These have one mind, and shall give their power and strength unto the beast.

14 These shall make war with the Lamb, and the Lamb shall overcome them: for he is Lord of lords, and King of kings: and they that are with him are called, and chosen, and faithful.

THE GREAT HYMN
ALL HAIL THE POWER OF JESUS NAME

All hail the pow'r of Jesus' Name!
Let angels prostrate fall;
Bring forth the royal diadem,
And crown Him Lord of all!

Bring forth the royal diadem
Ye chosen seed of Israel's race,
Ye ransomed from the fall,
Hail Him Who saves you by His grace,
And crown Him Lord of all!

Hail Him Who saves you by His grace,
And crown Him Lord of all!
You are Lord of all
You are Lord of all
Let every kindred, every tribe,
On this terrestrial ball,
To Him all majesty ascribe,
And crown Him Lord of all!

To Him all majesty ascribe,
And crown Him Lord of all!
And crown Him Lord of all!
And crown Him Lord of all!

God, so many thoughts come to mind when I consider who You are for me. There are days when I try to exhaust my ideas of You only to realize that You are more than what my finite mind can contain. You are a Father, a friend, a rock, a shelter, a doctor, a lawyer, a judge, a teacher, a prophet, a redeemer, a Savior, a priest, and, most of all, You are a KING. Lord, Your reign shall never end, Your counsel is perfect, Your glory is splendid, and Your decisions are flawless! Thank You, Jesus, for not being my elected President only serving one term; bless You for not being my appointed ambassador who only sits for a season—I praise You for being my KING and allowing me to be a subject in Your Kingdom! In Jesus' name I pray. Amen.

Article 10

THE GREAT HIM
JESUS IS KING OF KINGS
Revelation 17:1-14

by
Dr. Frederick D. Haynes III

James Baldwin was living through a dark moment in his life. American oppression of Black people had crushed dreams and set the stage for the assassinations of Medgar Evers, Malcolm X, and Martin Luther King Jr. Baldwin emerged from the nightmare of despair and chose life. According to Dr. Eddie Glaude Jr., in his book *Begin Again*, an interviewer for *Ebony* magazine asked Baldwin, "What, then, about hope?" Baldwin's response was this light of insight: "Hope is invented every day" (Glaude Jr., 2020, p. 145). Hope is especially vital for those who are oppressed and live with their "backs against the wall"—to use the language of Howard Thurman. Hope is a protest against the present that sets the stage for an alternative future. Hope may be illustrated by a character in the movie *Shawshank Redemption*, Andy Dufresne. Dufresne had been sentenced to life in prison for a crime he did not commit. He was a victim of injustice.

In one memorable scene, Dufresne is engaged in conversation with one of the respected leaders among the prisoners: Red. He oratorically takes flight on the wings of hope-filled imagination and shares with Red his vision of owning a hotel and a boat on a beach in Mexico. Life in Shawshank is characterized by vicious bullying, heartbreaking hardship, and oppressive control, but Andy Dufresne dares to invent hope every day. Dufresne imagines life beyond the intense immediacy of the iron hand of Shawshank suppression.

The recipients of the Apocalyptic Literature, known as the book of Revelation, had to learn how to invent hope every day. Their pastor, John, had been sentenced to Patmos to live out his days. They had been criminalized and otherized by the empire. They had felt the fiery breath of the dragon, and they knew all too well the bite of the beast. The followers of Jesus of Nazareth, who had been lynched by the Roman Empire, had been labeled enemies of the state. The believers in a resurrected Lord were treated as third-class citizens. Allan A. Boesak, in *Comfort and Protest*, says of the book of Revelation, "The suffering of Christians as a result of political oppression is the explicit theme. John himself has been banished to Patmos, a Christian by the name of Antipas is killed in Pergamum (Revelation 2:13), and there is evidence of more victims (6:8). Some have been beheaded (20:4). This kind of persecution makes it clear to John and the church that there is an enemy and that he is real, 'drunk with the blood of the saints and the blood of the martyrs of Jesus (17:6)'" (Boesak, 1987, p. 33). The Sitz im Leben of the recipients of Revelation is brutal political repression, economic exploitation, and bloodthirsty murder.

The attack on the early Christians was the result of their subversive claim that Jesus Christ, ALONE, is Lord. This Christological conviction put the Christian community on a collision course with the emperor and the empire. Boesak explains, "It is accepted that at the centre of the Apocalypse lies the issue of obedience and loyalty—to God or to the deified Caesar." He goes on to quote historian Karl Baus: "The pretext for the persecution in the eastern provinces was therefore based solely on the accusation of 'lese-majeste' which rejection of emperor worship involved" (Boesak, p. 24).

The book of Revelation is Apocalyptic Literature that infused the redeemed readers with a sense of anticipation and agitation or hope and protest. Revelation is a subversive prophetic protest against the present persecution of the Roman Empire that dares to envision an alternative future of victory and justice. The alternative future is ushered in by the resurrected Revolutionary, Jesus Christ, who is "King of kings and Lord of lords." As King of kings and Lord of lords, Jesus inspires His followers to invent hope every day.

Chapter 17 signals the fall of Babylon (symbolizing Rome). Babylon is portrayed as a whore who gains the allegiance of the populace through co-optation or coercion, according to Wes Howard-Brook and Anthony Gwyther in *Unveiling Empire: Then and Now*. They explain, "The Roman Empire employed various forms of execution both as means of eliminating those perceived as threatening the empire and as threats to keep people in line. This is why mass crucifixions occurred along public thoroughfares and on the tops of hills and why people were thrown to the wild animals in the arenas" (Howard-Brook and Gwyther, 1999, p. 170). The seven heads are the seven emperors, and the ten horns symbolize the power of the kings who make an alliance with Rome and attack the Lamb. However, verse 14 surprises the audience because "the Lamb shall overcome them: for he is Lord of lords, and King of kings." Jesus as King of kings is a political statement about the sovereignty of Jesus and a hope-filled belief in our victory in Jesus.

Jesus, as King of kings, is a subversive political proclamation. Caesar did not permit competition. The emperor Domitian had enforced his claim to divinity by law. He insisted on being addressed as "my Lord and my God." When John sees the Lamb defeating the kings, the beast, and the whore, and declares that it is because the Lamb is the King of Kings, this is prophetic hope that forecasts and reveals an alternative political future. The King of Kings is sovereign and will have the last word.

Jesus, as King of kings, fuels our hope in the midst of oppression that the fight is "fixed" because the upset victory of the Lamb over the oppressive empire and her allies is our victory. We identify with fans of sports teams who shout, "We won!" when their teams have experienced victory on the playing field. The fans have made a commitment to that team and so identify with the team that they claim the victory. Because Jesus is King of kings, those with their backs against the wall are inspired to invent hope every day.

THE GREAT HYMN
YES GOD IS REAL

There are some things I may not know
There are some places I can't go
But I'm sure Of this one thing
That God is real For I can feel
Him deep within

Yes, God is real, Real in my soul
Yes, God is real, For He has washed
And made me whole His love for me
Is like pure gold Yes, God is real
For I can feel Him in my soul

Some folks may doubt, Some folks may scorn
All can desert And leave me alone
But as for me I'll take God's part
For God is real and I can feel Him in my heart

I cannot tell Just how you felt
When Jesus took all your sins away
But since that day Yes, since that hour
God has been real For I can feel
His holy power

DR. MARK "DEAN" HAYWOOD
Grace School of Theology
Houston, Texas

DR. MARK "DEAN" HAYWOOD
GRACE SCHOOL OF THEOLOGY
HOUSTON, TEXAS

JESUS IS THE INDESCRIBABLE GIFT
2 Corinthians 9:1-15

1 For as touching the ministering to the saints, it is superfluous for me to write to you:

2 For I know the forwardness of your mind, for which I boast of you to them of Macedonia, that Achaia was ready a year ago; and your zeal hath provoked very many.

3 Yet have I sent the brethren, lest our boasting of you should be in vain in this behalf; that, as I said, ye may be ready:

4 Lest haply if they of Macedonia come with me, and find you unprepared, we (that we say not, ye) should be ashamed in this same confident boasting.

5 Therefore I thought it necessary to exhort the brethren, that they would go before unto you, and make up beforehand your bounty, whereof ye had notice before, that the same might be ready, as a matter of bounty, and not as of covetousness.

6 But this I say, He which soweth sparingly shall reap also sparingly; and he which soweth bountifully shall reap also bountifully.

7 Every man according as he purposeth in his heart, so let him give; not grudgingly, or of necessity: for God loveth a cheerful giver.

8 And God is able to make all grace abound toward you; that ye, always having all sufficiency in all things, may abound to every good work:

9 (As it is written, He hath dispersed abroad; he hath given to the poor: his righteousness remaineth for ever.

10 Now he that ministereth seed to the sower both minister bread for your food, and multiply your seed sown, and increase the fruits of your righteousness;)

11 Being enriched in every thing to all bountifulness, which causeth through us thanksgiving to God.

12 For the administration of this service not only supplieth the want of the saints, but is abundant also by many thanksgivings unto God;

13 Whiles by the experiment of this ministration they glorify God for your professed subjection unto the gospel of Christ, and for your liberal distribution unto them, and unto all men;

14 And by their prayer for you, which long after you for the exceeding grace of God in you.

15 Thanks be unto God for his unspeakable gift.

THE GREAT HYMN
A MIGHTY FORTRESS IS OUR GOD

A mighty fortress is our God,
a bulwark never failing;
our helper he, amid the flood
of mortal ills prevailing.
For still our ancient foe
does seek to work us woe;
his craft and power are great,
and armed with cruel hate,
on earth is not his equal.

Did we in our own strength confide,
our striving would be losing,
were not the right Man on our side,
the Man of God's own choosing.
You ask who that may be?
Christ Jesus, it is he;
Lord Sabaoth his name,
from age to age the same;

That Word above all earthly powers
no thanks to them abideth;
the Spirit and the gifts are ours
through him who with us sideth.
Let goods and kindred go,
this mortal life also;
the body they may kill:
God's truth abideth still;
his kingdom is forever!

O Lord, You are, without a doubt, the greatest gift that I have ever received in my life. You meet all of my needs, You hear and answer my prayers and petitions, and You provide and care for me in every possible way. With this in heart, I lift this prayer to You in sincere and devout thanksgiving. I bow to You because Your consolation and love often overwhelm me and leave me with an endless feeling of unending indebtedness to You. Thank You, Lord Jesus, for being the gift that keeps on giving. It is in Your name that I petition heaven with this praise. Amen.

Article 11

THE GREAT HIM
JESUS IS THE INDESCRIBABLE GIFT
2 Corinthians 9:1-15

by
Dr. Mark Haywood

Pastor Tillmon knows about receiving incredible gifts from God. Pastor Kerry W. Tillmon is a good friend of mine and ministry partner. He has served as pastor of West Point Baptist Church in Galveston, Texas, for the past thirty-five years. During his tenure at the church, God blessed him and his wife with a senior citizen named Sister Early Evans. Sister Evans is a culinary artist, and each Sunday, she shares her cooking prowess with Pastor and his family. What makes her an incredible gift from God is that she has performed this ministry for thirty-five years without interruption. Additionally, she feeds all the visiting Sunday morning preachers who accompany Pastor and his family. Sister Evans was sixty-five when she started supporting Pastor Tillmon and recently celebrated her 100th birthday. Because she is a member and servant of another church, this makes her service to Tillmon's ministry even more incredible.

I had the distinct pleasure of enjoying her culinary skills when I substituted for Pastor Tillmon during August and September of 2020. It was clear that Sister Evans is an incredible gift from God. As observers of Sister Evans, we can clearly and adequately describe her efforts and conclude that she is an incredible gift from God. Conversely, in the epigraph cited above, the apostle Paul does not write about an incredible gift but the "indescribable gift" from God found in Jesus Christ, who is the focus of this article. Further, the evidence contained herein is not designed to be exhaustive but illustrative of Jesus as our "indescribable gift" from God.

Based on Paul's statement, we are encouraged to thank God and realize that Jesus Christ is the "indescribable gift." The Greek word for "indescribable" is *anēkdiētos*, which the lexicon BDAG defines as "indescribable in the good sense"; the *Vocabulary of the Greek Testament* by Mouton and Milligan defines it as "wonderful beyond description"; and the *Englishman's Concordance* translates the word as "unspeakable." Each author proffers the concept that God's gift (Jesus the Christ) is beyond human explanation.

The other key term that must be considered for this discourse is the word *gift* (*dōrea*). Here, BDAG defines it in the following manner: "that which is given or transferred freely by one person to another, gift, bounty, of God." In other words, you cannot work for a gift, you do not deserve it, it is not a bribe, and there are no strings attached to it. You need only receive Him (God's gift of Jesus)—and believing is receiving!

So, what makes Jesus our indescribable gift? The answer is found in apostle Paul's polemic as well as the person and work of Christ. First, Paul's polemic lies within the biblical context addressed in 2 Corinthians, chapters 8 and 9. At first blush, this seems odd because chapters 8 and 9 delineate Paul's efforts to collect an offering for the poverty-stricken Hebrew Christians in Jerusalem (see Romans 15:26). To this end, apostle Paul solicited funds from those Christians living outside of Palestine. For example, he requested a grace offering from Christians residing in Galatia (see 1 Corinthians 16:1), Macedonia (see Acts 19:22; 2 Corinthians 8:1-5; 9:2, 4), Achaia (see Romans 15:26; 1 Corinthians 16:13-16; 2 Corinthians 9), and Asia Minor (see Acts 20:35; Acts 24:17-18). Several representatives from these locales returned to Jerusalem with Paul (see Acts 20:4). One of Paul's goals and objectives was to institute a philosophy of Christian stewardship among the saints. In 1 Corinthians 9:15, Paul presented the concept by indicating that if God could give the "indescribable gift" to the world, then believers should respond with a gracious monetary gift to Jerusalem's poor saints. This was a form of thanking God for granting the "indescribable gift" of Jesus Christ. In short, Jesus is the gift from God that is the impetus for believers' offering all categories of gifts to benefit God and others.

Second, Jesus Christ's person and ministry work set forth reasons why He is the "indescribable gift." Now, because of restrictions placed on this article coupled with the voluminous attributes of Jesus, I will briefly address seven key areas that underscore Jesus as the "indescribable gift." They include the protoevangelium, the Angel of the Lord, His incarnation, His humiliation, His crucifixion, His exaltation, and His ultimate coronation. The *protoevangelium* is defined as the first gospel found in Genesis 3:15, where God judged the serpent and prophesied that the woman's seed would bruise the head of the serpent (total defeat), with the serpent bruising (via Crucifixion) His heel. Scholars identify Jesus as the "seed of the woman" and the serpent as Satan. Thus, in the first book of the Bible, God promised that Jesus would defeat Satan by way of the Cross. Now, that's incredible and indescribable!

Next, Jesus is the Angel of the Lord (AoL), who is the pre-incarnate Christ ministering in the Old Testament before He was born in a manger to Mary and Joseph. As you read Genesis 18:1-15, the AoL visits Abraham and Sarah, along with two angels in the form of men. (See Genesis 19:1, 15 or Exodus 3:1-22.) In other words, Christ existed before Jesus came through His mother, Mary, who is called "the mother of God" (*Theotokos*). How do you explain that exhaustively? When you arrive in the New Testament, you find the incarnation of Jesus, where He adds humanity to His deity. This is called the "Hypostatic Union," revealing Jesus as all-God, all-man—all at the same time. (See John 1:1-18; Romans 1:1-4; Philippians 2:5-8; and Hebrews 1:1-13.) This is another inexplicable attribute of our Lord, in that He restricted Himself as He so desired in order to feel what we feel and to suffer on our behalf. (See John 11:35; 2 Corinthians 5:21; Hebrews 4:15.) Jesus confounded the religious leaders with the Incarnation when He asked, "Therefore David himself calls Him 'Lord'; how is He then his Son?" (Mark 12:37, NKJV). Expressed in a different way, how can Christ exist as David's subordinate (son) and superior (Lord) simultaneously? (See Psalm 110:1; Mark 12:35-37.) Of course, such a concept is confusing at best as well as indescribable.

Lastly, a careful reading of Philippians 2:5-11 manifests Jesus' humiliation (He became a servant), His crucifixion (substitutionary atonement where He died in our place), His exaltation by God (highly honored), and His ultimate coronation (crowned the King of Kings, Revelation 19:16). Each one of these attributes of Jesus Christ will result in every knee's bowing, and every tongue's confessing that Jesus is Lord, to the glory of God the Father. What an "indescribable gift" we have from God! In summary, this article has merely scratched the surface regarding Jesus as the "indescribable gift" because of time limitations and space. The information contained herein is not designed to be exhaustive but illustrative of Jesus as our "indescribable gift" from God. Moreover, the apostle Paul, in 2 Corinthians 9:15, and other biblical authors have proffered overwhelming evidence for why Jesus is the "indescribable gift" from God.

THE GREAT HYMN
COME THOU FOUNT OF EVERY BLESSING

Come, Thou Fount of every blessing
Tune my heart to sing Thy grace
Streams of mercy, never ceasing
Call for songs of loudest praise

Teach me some melodious sonnet
Sung by flaming tongues above
Praise the mount, I'm fixed upon it
Mount of Thy redeeming love

Here I raise my Ebenezer
Here there by Thy great help I've come
And I hope, by Thy good pleasure
Safely to arrive at home

Jesus sought me when a stranger
Wandering from the fold of God
He, to rescue me from danger
Interposed His precious blood

Oh, that day when freed from sinning
I shall see Thy lovely face
Clothed then in the blood washed linen
How I'll sing Thy wondrous grace

Come, my Lord, no longer tarry
Take my ransomed soul away
Send Thine angels now to carry
Me to realms of endless...

PASTOR DENNIS C. JONES
Gethsemane Missionary Baptist Church
Houston, Texas

PASTOR DENNIS C. JONES
GETHSEMANE MISSIONARY BAPTIST CHURCH
HOUSTON, TEXAS

JESUS IS THE ROCK
1 Corinthians 10:1-4

1 Moreover, brethren, I would not that ye should be ignorant, how that all our fathers were under the cloud, and all passed through the sea;

2 And were all baptized unto Moses in the cloud and in the sea;

3 And did all eat the same spiritual meat;

4 And did all drink the same spiritual drink: for they drank of that spiritual Rock that followed them: and that Rock was Christ.

THE GREAT HYMN
ROCK OF AGES

Rock of ages cleft for me let me hide myself in Thee
Let the water and the blood from Thy wounded
side which fload
Thee of sin the double cure save from raft
and make me pure
Let me hide myself in Thee

In my hand no prize I bring simply to Thy cross I cling
While I draw this pleading breath when
my eyes shall close in death
Lord when I rise to world unknown and behold
the on Thy throne
Rock of ages cleft for me let me hime myself in Thee
Let me hide myself in Thee

Lord, the times we live in seem perilous and problematic. Nothing seems stable. Everything seems to be so volatile—thus the purpose of this petition. God, You have always been our rock, our place of stability, the one on whom we could depend and lean when all else fails. Thank You, Jesus, for being all that You are each moment for those who believe. The prayer that comes with this supplication is simply this: help us hold on to You when it seems that You are all that we have to hold on to. In the name of Jesus Christ I pray. Amen!

Article 12

**THE GREAT HIM
JESUS IS THE ROCK
1 Corinthians 10:1-4**

**by
Pastor Dennis C. Jones**

The lesson of 1 Corinthians 10 teaches us that what the rock was to Israel physically, Jesus is to us spiritually. He uses Israel's nation to show the Church how the improper use of freedom could render a person ineffective in service to Christ and the Church. The children of Israel gave Paul illustrations of some dangers of conceited living. Paul is comparing the presumptuous attitude of God's people under Moses to the arrogance of certain Corinthian Christians in his day. To prove his point, Paul used some situations from the forty years when Israel wandered in the wilderness. He opens the chapter in this manner to show that some of Israel was disqualified from entering the Promised Land. Paul did not want the Corinthians to make the same mistake. The reason why many Christians are spiritually empty is that they have not realized that God's lessons from the past help us to live in the present. What was written in the past is as relevant today as it was when it was written.

God brought Israel across the Red Sea on dry land. He guided them by a pillar of cloud by day and a pillar of fire by night. The pillar of cloud and the pillar of fire that guided the Israelites by day and night were God's presence. Paul said the children of Israel were baptized into Moses because they identified with him as their leader over them. Paul wanted the Corinthians to know that the source of Israel's blessings was God. This was a reminder of the fact that their blessings were spiritual and not material. Jesus Christ is the spiritual rock who followed Israel and provided them with their blessings. The water from the rock happened in Exodus 17 when Israel was camped at a place called Rephidim. Since there was no water to drink, the people complained to Moses, and Moses cried to the Lord. God instructed Moses to strike a particular rock, and water would come out of it that the people may drink. Don't ever think that being set free from bondage means being free from difficulty. Trouble and trials are part of the Christian life necessary for our growth. The fact that problems come on the path of obedience needs repeated emphasis because of the delusions about God's way. Many seem to have the idea that if you are obeying God in your walk, then your life will be peaches and cream. Show me the Christian close to the Lord, and I will show you the one who has had his or her share of problems.

The text does not give any specific purpose for this trial, but God never sends a test without a good reason. Water is a necessity, and when Jehovah takes His people where there is no water to drink, it must be under the compulsion of a higher necessity. Our physical needs are essential, but our spiritual needs are far more critical. God's primary interest in humankind is the soul. Everything else He does for us is extra. Any time the Israelites had a concern, they started complaining. There are a lot of people who go through life standing at the complaint counter. When God does not do what we think He ought to do in the way we think He ought to do it, we complain about it. The way some people find fault, you would think there was a reward. Do not pray for rain if you are going to complain about mud. Anything God brings us to, He can carry us through.

Even though God was there, the people could not get their eyes off their problem long enough to see Him. The question is, how far have you traveled from Rephidim? This is more than a question of geography; it is a question of spiritual growth. Too many in the body of Christ seem to be still at Rephidim. We still doubt God's presence, which we all tend to do when we want something and cannot seem to get it. Had they believed He was among them, they would have been restored in the assurance that He who had brought them out of Egypt, parted the waters of the Red Sea, delivered them from the hand of Pharaoh, and guided them in all their journeys by the pillar of cloud by day and the pillar of fire by night would in His own time hear their cry and supply their need. I believe that God's performance in the past should give us peace in the present. The deity of God was about both His presence and His power. These same people had already received significant evidence of His presence with them and His power for them. The plagues in Israel, the Red Sea crossing, the bitter water made sweet at Marah, and the daily supply of manna were all great pieces of evidence of God's presence and power. Still, they wondered whether He was there for them. Their unbelief was unbelievable. "How soon we forget" should be written over all of us. Their simple prayer should have been, "Lord, do it again." This was the most unlikely place to get water and reminds us, again, that God can provide for us regardless of the circumstances around us. We may see no means of help, but God is not limited to our usual, customary, or logical means.

When the people were thirsty, God showed Moses the rock. The blessing of the text is in the definite article "the." It was not a rock, but The Rock. Jesus was not one of many saviors—He is THE SAVIOR OF THE WORLD. Divine Revelation informed Moses where the saving Rock was and what he was to do to get water. Like the Gospel, this plan would never have been invented by human beings. It had to be revealed by God to humanity. The term "rock of Horeb" indicated that in the area of the southern portion of the Sinai Peninsula was a rock known as the rock of Horeb. However, merely knowing that the rock existed would do nothing to save the Israelites. In other words, the divine revelation did not inform Moses how the rock could solve the water problem. If Christ is to save us, then we need more knowledge about Christ than the fact that Christ existed; we need divine revelation to tell us that Christ can save us and how He can save us.

The Christ of history must become the Christ of reality. The written Word must become the living Word. Jehovah, God, came down to earth and stood on the rock of Horeb. He came to earth to be our Savior. He dwelt among the sons of men as a man in person that spiritually is represented by the meaning of the word *Horeb*, the place where the rock was located. The Hebrew word translated *Horeb* means "dry, desert, barren and desolate." Those words describe the spiritual situation on the globe. It is a fitting picture of people without Christ. Yet, the Lord can bring forth life out of emptiness. John 7:38 (NKJV) reads, "He who believes in Me, as the Scripture has said, out of his heart will flow rivers of living water." Christ is present both in person and in symbol. In this illustration, Christ the Lord stands on the rock as the angel, but the rock's symbol is needed to provide the parallel of human nature to which he must receive the atoning blow of judgment.

A great deal of controversy was caused over the fact that He was both God and human. Many would not accept the fact that Mary's baby was also God's Son. Mary's baby got thirsty, but God's Son told the Samaritan woman, "I am living water." Mary's baby got hungry, but God's Son fed a multitude. Mary's baby went to sleep on a ship, but God's Son calmed the storm. Mary's baby rode a ship, but God's Son walked on water. Mary's baby cried at a grave, but God's Son raised Lazarus from the dead. The rock teaches us that Jesus was a revelation of God, not a creation of God. There was never a time when He did not exist. John 1:1-3 reads, "In the beginning was the Word, and the Word was with God, and the Word was God. The same was in the beginning with God. All things were made by him; and without him was not any thing made that was made." Jesus, in His original form, existed before He was born in Bethlehem. It was Jesus who visited Abraham in Genesis 18. It was Jesus who wrestled with Jacob in Genesis 32. It was Jesus who was the fourth man in the fiery furnace in Daniel 3. He had to become what we are to make us what He is. The Son of God became the Son of man, so we, the sons of men, might become God's sons.

If you stumble over the Incarnation, you will stumble over the Creation. At Creation, God took a woman from the rib of a man. At the Incarnation, God took a man from the womb of a woman. God took Jesus and fashioned Himself into a real man who could live next door. The Holy Ghost conceived Jesus in the womb of Mary without human help. Because He had a dateless past, He had to borrow time from Himself to get from eternity to time. He made a world before He visited it. He made His mother before she conceived Him. He has a birthday but never gets old. Demonstration of His crucifixion is seen when Moses struck the rock. This was necessary to receive the water. Likewise, Jesus had to be smitten so that we might receive the forgiveness of our sins.

Once smitten, He never needs to be smitten again. All we have to do is speak to the rock, and the water of life will flow freely. They could have leaned on that rock, talked to that rock, placed their empty cups up to that rock and cried out, "Come out, water!" and they would have died from thirst if the rock had never been struck. Had the rock never received the blow, they would not have had water to save them. We are not saved by parables or miracles, but by the crucified Savior. Apostates do not want to view calvary as a necessity but only as an unfortunate event. But unless Christ dies for our sins, we will have no blessed Gospel to preach. Isaiah 53 reads, "He was wounded for our transgressions. He was bruised for our iniquities. The chastisement of our peace is upon him, and with his stripes, we are healed." In Numbers 20, Moses missed the Promised Land because he smote the rock when he was told to speak to the rock. One crucifixion was enough for our salvation. Now we have the privilege of speaking to the Rock. *Now, let us have a little talk with Jesus. Let us tell Him all about our troubles. He will hear our faintest cry, and He will answer by and by. And when you feel a little prayer wheel turnin', and you know a little fire is burnin'. Find a little talk with Jesus makes it right.*

The Rock was not smitten for itself but for the salvation of the people. He paid a debt He did not owe because we owed a debt we could not pay. The hymn writer reminds us Jesus paid it all. All to Him I owe. Sin has left a crimson stain, but He washed it white as snow. The glory of this water is that it did not come with a water bill. Isaiah 55 reads, "Ho, every one that thirsteth, come ye to the waters, and he that hath no money; come ye, buy and eat; yea, come, buy wine and milk without money and without price." The water from the rock reminds us that we can trust in God's providence for our daily needs. We can trust in God's Son for our deepest needs.

Thirst was the only physical suffering that Christ ever acknowledged in His earthly sojourn. That acknowledgment came on the Cross when He said, "I thirst"—and that thirst represents the worst thirst problem of all: the thirst that lost souls will have in hell's fire. Even though the water that was given in grace was free, it would not do any good if the people did not drink the water. The water had to be received by the body if the person was going to be saved. In like manner, though soul salvation is wonderful, it will do no good if a person does not receive Christ as Savior.

In verse 4, Paul says that the same rock followed them. The glory of this verse is that the Lord not only appears at our salvation, but also, He abides in our preservation. John 14:16 reads, "And I will pray the Father, and he shall give you another Comforter, that he may abide with you for ever." This is why we sing, "Amazing grace, how sweet the sound that saved a wretch like me. I once was lost, but now am found; was blind, but now I see." That's our salvation. But we also sing, "Through many dangers, toils and snares, I have already come. Twas grace that brought me safe thus far, and grace will lead me on." That's our preservation. Our survival does not depend on our fickleness but on the Lord's faithfulness. The Lord is faithful. Hebrews 13:8 reads, "Jesus Christ the same yesterday, and to day, and for ever."

Men change, customs change—but Christ never changes. The presence of God was such a blessing that Moses did not want to move if the presence of God would not go with them. All of us should value the privilege of God's presence as highly as Moses did. A perfect picture of the Christian's sojourn is found in Matthew 14. Jesus put the disciples in a boat while He went to the mountain to pray. While we sail the seas of life, Jesus is praying for us. The human tendency in trouble is to picture God with blind eyes. The disciples were out of His presence but not out of His sight. It does not matter whether we see Him; all that matters is that He sees us. So, I sing because I am happy. I sing because I am free. His eye is on the sparrow, and I know He watches over me. No storm can hide us where God cannot find us. Just as surely as the Lord is in control of the sunshine, He is also in control of the storm.

THE GREAT HYMN
THE SOLID ROCK

My hope is built on nothing less
Than Jesus' blood and righteousness;
I dare not trust the sweetest frame,
But wholly lean on Jesus' name.

Refrain:

On Christ, the solid Rock, I stand;
All other ground is sinking sand,
All other ground is sinking sand.

When darkness veils His lovely face,
I rest on His unchanging grace;
In every high and stormy gale,
My anchor holds within the veil.

His oath, His covenant, His blood
Support me in the whelming flood;
When all around my soul gives way,
He then is all my hope and stay.

When He shall come with trumpet sound,
Oh, may I then in Him be found;
Dressed in His righteousness alone,
Faultless to stand before the throne

PASTOR PAUL D. LANDREW
Loving Word Fellowship Church
Houston, Texas

PASTOR PAUL D. LANDREW
LOVING WORD FELLOWSHIP CHURCH
HOUSTON, TEXAS

JESUS IS THE SON OF THE MOST HIGH

Luke 1:28-32

28 And the angel came in unto her, and said, Hail, thou that art highly favoured, the Lord is with thee: blessed art thou among women.

29 And when she saw him, she was troubled at his saying, and cast in her mind what manner of salutation this should be.

30 And the angel said unto her, Fear not, Mary: for thou hast found favour with God.

31 And, behold, thou shalt conceive in thy womb, and bring forth a son, and shalt call his name Jesus.

32 He shall be great, and shall be called the Son of the Highest: and the Lord God shall give unto him the throne of his father David.

THE GREAT HYMN
HOLY, HOLY, HOLY

Holy, holy, holy
Lord, God Almighty
Early in the morning our song shall rise to Thee
Holy, holy, holy
Merciful and mighty
God in three persons blessed Trinity

Holy, holy, holy
Though the darkness hide Thee
Though the eye of sinful man thy glory may not see
Only Thou art holy; there is none beside Thee
Perfect in power, in love, and purity

Holy, holy, holy
Lord, God Almighty
All Thy works shall praise Thy name in earth and sky and sea
Holy, holy, holy
Merciful and mighty
God in three persons blessed Trinity

There are none like You, O God, none like You. When I consider the heavens and all of its splendor, there are none like You. When I consider the beautiful, heightened hills that stand majestically over the plains of our human existence—when I consider the bounty of Your grace, the matchless care of Your mercy, and the inexplicable nature of Your love, it compels my heart to cry in prayer. There are none like You, O God. Lord, thank You for being the only celebrity in the universe. I bow my knee to You now as Lord, and I lift my heart to You in praise because You and You alone are worthy. In Jesus' name I pray. Amen.

Article 13

THE GREAT HIM
JESUS IS THE SON OF THE MOST HIGH
Luke 1:28-32

by
Pastor Paul D. Landrew

Most people have had the experience of meeting someone in person for the first time without the benefit of a mutual acquaintance. The meetings are typically made successful because of each party's willingness to share some distinguishing feature or attribute about himself/herself. The shared attribute allows the parties to distinguish themselves among all the other available people in the meeting place.

In Luke 1:32, the Son of the Highest is both introduced and presented to the world. With an inexhaustible, available list of attributes, Luke captures the angel's identifier word to the virgin mother. She is told, "He shall be called Son of the Highest." This description is atypical, since it recalls the aspect of relative comparison instead of character identity. It not only presents Jesus but also positions Him. We are immediately presented with the reality that although He has come for us, He is not like us.

But why "the Highest"? There is something about height that affects people differently. Those who tend to live on the extreme edge of challenge and adventure—seemingly with ease—defy the harsh reality of their feet's being high above the ground. They move with courageous caution as they climb cliffs or mountains, scale buildings, and traverse high wires. Their focus seems to override the ever-present danger of a misstep, miscalculation, or unanticipated circumstance. Others are not so daring; they respect height from the ground. They are confident in the control they have on the solid surface. The power of height, however, is not lost on them. The soaring trees and majestic mountains create in them an awe-inspiring emotion. They are aware of the beauty of height and choose to enjoy it from a more stable setting. Such a diverse and impacting reality of height on the minds of men and women can give us a glimpse of why God would use it as a descriptive attribute of Himself.

While seemingly without the ability to be quantified, this name *Highest* challenges us in a tangible way to reverence three critical attributes of God. They are His Majesty, His Mindset, and His Methods. These attributes embody how the Highest gives the climber and the walker the same opportunity to be awed by Him. The Bible reveals God; there is no more incredible testimony of His majesty than the words "In the beginning God." God, unlike man, exists and is without cause, creation, and comparison. A. W. Tozer says, "God dwells in His creation and is everywhere indivisibly present in all His works. He is transcendent above all His works even while He is immanent within them."

Psalm 8 and Psalm 19 work in unison to confirm that the heavens are the eyewitness to the Glory of God. The Highest, which has not been experienced by temporal man in place of His resident Glory, has had His testimony come from the nearest witness. An easy blending of Psalm 8:3 and Psalm 19:1 (ESV) echo this reality: "When I look at your heavens, the work of your fingers, the moon and the stars, which you have set in place, . . . the heavens declare the glory of God, and the sky above proclaims his handiwork." That which cannot be reached fully by man holds a front-row seat to the Majesty of God. To investigate the moon's face and the stars is to stare in the face of God's witnesses. The Majesty of God is more remarkable when you understand that astronauts, hikers, and scuba divers are all granted access to His Majestic Height. We are not denied admission because of spiritual acrophobia. The Highest invaded time and did so to become accessible to those who would seek Him from their vantage point.

Next, His chosen entrance into the world gives us a behind-the-scenes glimpse of His Mindset. We are, according to Psalm 139:14, "fearfully and wonderfully made"—while Psalm 8:4 (NKJV) asks the question, "What is man that You are mindful of him, and the son of man that You visit him?" The Highest visits without discrimination or concern of our current state and infiltrates the conditions of men without partiality. He arrives not only at the welcoming gifts of the societal elite—wise men—but also to the warmth of the meekest of the social structure: shepherds.

In truth, the mindset of the Highest comes near to us as we experience His methods. His thoughts are higher than ours, so are His ways higher than ours. The methods of the Highest can reveal great mercy when He acts. Because He has chosen among infinite possibilities, options, and alternatives, His methods are without flaw. He sits above creation, so all that creation offers is simply the Highest gift back to Himself. He works in high places to do great things for the low, the ordinary, and the pedestrian. He used Ararat (16,946 feet) as the docking marina for the ark. He used Horeb (6,460 feet) as the writing gallery of Moses. He used Mount Carmel (1,791 feet) as Elijah's battleground with idolatry. He used Olivet (2,710 feet) as the launching pad of the Savior to His place on the right hand of the Highest. But He used Golgotha, called Calvary (2,520 feet, a four-story climb from base to top) to hold a cross to pay our debt and redeem our souls. The "Son of the Highest" permitted His handiworks to have His body until our debt was paid. And then He cried, "It is Finished!"

John Muir said, "We are now in the mountains, and they are in us, kindling enthusiasm, making every nerve quiver, filling every pore and cell of us." Because of the work of the Highest, we can say, "We are now in the Highest, and the Highest is in us, kindling us to new life, raising the thought standards of our minds and filling every void ever created by sin.

THE GREAT HYMN
CROWN HIM WITH MANY CROWNS

Crown Him with many crowns,
The lamb upon the throne:
Hark! How the heav'nly anthem drowns
All Music but its own!

Awake, my soul, and sing
Of Him who died for thee,
And hail him as thy matchless King
Through all eternity.

Crown Him with many crowns
Crown Him with many crowns
Crown Him the Lord of Heav'n:
One with the Father known.
One with the Spirit through Him giv'n

From yonder glorious throne.
To Thee be endless praise.
For Thou hast died for me;
Be Thou, O Lord, through endless days
Adored and magnified
Adored and magnified

Crown Him with many crowns
His glories now we sing,
Who died and rose on high,
Who died eternal life to bring
And, lives that death may die.
Crown Him with many crowns

BISHOP RUDOLPH W. McKISSICK JR.
The Bethel Experience
Jacksonville, Florida

BISHOP RUDOLPH W. McKISSICK, JR.
THE BETHEL EXPERIENCE
JACKSONVILLE, FLORIDA

JESUS IS THE LIGHT OF THE WORLD

John 8:1-12

1 Jesus went unto the mount of Olives.

2 And early in the morning he came again into the temple, and all the people came unto him; and he sat down, and taught them.

3 And the scribes and Pharisees brought unto him a woman taken in adultery; and when they had set her in the midst,

4 They say unto him, Master, this woman was taken in adultery, in the very act.

5 Now Moses in the law commanded us, that such should be stoned: but what sayest thou?

6 This they said, tempting him, that they might have to accuse him. But Jesus stooped down, and with his finger wrote on the ground, as though he heard them not.

7 So when they continued asking him, he lifted up himself, and said unto them, He that is without sin among you, let him first cast a stone at her.

8 And again he stooped down, and wrote on the ground.

9 And they which heard it, being convicted by their own conscience, went out one by one, beginning at the eldest, even unto the last: and Jesus was left alone, and the woman standing in the midst.

10 When Jesus had lifted up himself, and saw none but the woman, he said unto her, Woman, where are those thine accusers? hath no man condemned thee?

11 She said, No man, Lord. And Jesus said unto her, Neither do I condemn thee: go, and sin no more.

12 Then spake Jesus again unto them, saying, I am the light of the world: he that followeth me shall not walk in darkness, but shall have the light of life.

THE GREAT HYMN
JESUS THE LIGHT OF THE WORLD

Hark! the herald angels sing,
Jesus, the light of the world.
Glory to the newborn King,
Jesus, the light of the world.

We'll walk in the light, beautiful light.
Come where the dewdrops of mercy shine bright.
O, shine all around us by day and by night.
Jesus, the light of the world. Joyful, all you nations, rise.
Jesus, the light of the world. Join the triumph of the skies.
Jesus, the light of the world.

Christ, by highest heaven adored;
Jesus, the light of the world.
Christ, the everlasting Lord;
Jesus, the light of the world.
Hail, the heaven-born Prince of Peace!
Jesus, the light of the world.
Hail, the Sun of Righteousness!
Jesus, the light of the world.

O God, there are times when the darkness is so thick it is impossible not to see. Moral collapse, racial hatred, systemic evil, global poverty, pandemics, and infirmity are just everyday issues that now confront us. It is dark right now. What used to be right is wrong, and what used to be wrong is now right. Truth has been relativized, and there seems to be no regard for anything—to include the sanctity of human life itself. But Your light still shines bright! Light our path on earth with Your brilliant glory from heaven. Thank You, Jesus, for being our light that shines brightest when there seems to be no light at all near us. In the name of Jesus Christ I pray. Amen.

Article 14

THE GREAT HIM
JESUS IS THE LIGHT OF THE WORLD
John 8:1-12

by
Bishop Rudolph W. McKissick Jr.

John Ryan, president of the Center for Creative Leadership, writes, "Success always starts with vision." He further states that compelling visions can change the world but staying invested in them can be extremely difficult when hard times arrive. Then Ryan adds this critical statement in his missive. He says when it comes to living out a vision, persistence matters just as much as inspiration. He said to never promote the prize at the expense of hiding the price. It takes perseverance to realize dreams, goals, and visions.

Another writer once said that vision without action is a dream, and action without vision is merely passing the time. One of my favorite authors, Jonathan Swift, says that vision is the art of seeing what is invisible to others. Vision is the "seeing" in the already what your eyes will behold in the not yet. In other words, my eyes do not yet see it, but with my FAITH and sanctified imagination, it's in the already. Many people will never see anything—not because they don't have eyes, but because they don't have a vision.

YOU WILL NEVER GO FURTHER THAN YOUR VISION. The greatest weapon you have against mediocrity is vision. Vision provides clarity. Clarity allows focus. Focus gives confidence. Confidence encourages action. Action produces results. The question might be asked, what does this have to do with this Christological affirmation Jesus makes here in this chapter? One can't have vision when he or she is in the proverbial dark. Darkness does not just represent chronological darkness. In a very symbolic and metaphorical way, it means uncertainty and a lack of clarity.

Such is what the first-century Judaic leadership and the Jews had when it came to Jesus. Right from the beginning of John's gospel, John attempts to establish what the Jews and their leaders did not want to hear or believe—that Jesus was indeed not just a representative of God but was, in fact, God, God's self. John deliberately opens his gospel with an allusion to the Creation account's opening words in Genesis 1. Through the mystery of incarnation, the Word (who created the world) entered into the creation and became one of us. The God who exists as Spirit now and forever has become the God-man, God wrapped in flesh—fully human and fully Divine, without the necessity of an on-off switch.

What we see in the Creation story is a God of creativity and innovation. It should not be surprising, then, that this God who infused creation with change and innovation should then be innovative in His dealings with humanity. In His innovation, Jesus repeatedly tried to give understanding to His origin and identity and purpose through "I am" statements. These "I am" statements not only provide descriptors of purpose but also once again harken back to a familiar scene with God. It happens in Exodus 3. Moses, that Ebony emancipator and liberating lawgiver, asks God a question concerning the identity of God. Having been on the backside of the mountain for some time now, living in obscurity, Moses did not know who this God was. In turn, Moses needed to know who God is by name, knowing that going to Egypt and making claims of one God to a polytheistic culture would receive some scrutiny. God, in turn, tells Moses, *Who I am is too exhaustive to be minimized, defined, confined, or labeled with one answer. So, Moses, just tell them I AM THAT I AM is who I AM. In other words, who I am is determined by where you are and what you are in that calls for My intervention. And whoever I need to be to combat THAT . . . THAT I AM. Then when I have dealt with THAT, you can name Me descriptively based upon what I did in that situation.*

- I AM . . . a provider—because when you could not provide for yourself, I became your provision source.
- I AM a way out of no way—because when you did not know the way or thought there was no way, I became the way.
- I AM the Good Shepherd—because when you didn't know which way to go or strayed away, I was your guide.
- I AM the door—because I am the conduit from one place, one season, one reality to the next.

And here in this chapter, we see another I AM spoken from the mouth of the Master: I AM THE LIGHT. This one is the most significant to me for several reasons. One reason is that it takes us back to the very first thing God does. This concept of "light" was first mentioned creatively but is now said in a salvific and existential manner. In calling Himself "the Light," Jesus is submitting to them and to us that He is the way out of confusion, unclarity, mismanagement, and everything that keeps us from vision and clarity.

In the context of the text, it is evident from how the verse starts that this is a continuation of a previous scene. Many scholars debate the validity of the story that precedes this statement, which is the woman caught in adultery. With or without it, the point remains the same. Prior to that story, chapter 7 ends with division over who Jesus is and claims to be. Jesus speaks to them as if He has some divine authority, which is perplexing to both the Jews and their leaders because, in their eyes, He is neither God nor Messiah. He then is tested by them with this woman caught in adultery and forgives her of her sin, which not only becomes an ocular demonstration of HIS point but a further exacerbation of theirs. In their eyes, nobody has the authority to forgive sins BUT GOD. Their continued lack of clarity and vision then leads to this I AM statement: I AM THE LIGHT.

Several things about light: In practically every room in a home or an office or any building, there are lights. No matter how dark the room, perhaps the darkness is not evidence of the lack of the presence of light. The light is there, even in the darkness. The difference is that the present light can only be made active when you flip the switch. The flipping of the switch does not happen because you "just became aware" of the presence of the light. You flipped the switch because you didn't want to be in the darkness and could not maneuver in the darkness; you flipped the switch to activate the presence of the light so that the darkness went away. In a real sense, the darkness does not go away; the light just overpowers it.

Jesus was saying to those leaders and Jews, *You only are remaining in the dark by choice. The light is present with you. Your darkness is a choice. If you would just flip the switch of faith and let Me be to darkness who I can be, then the darkness would lose its power in your life.* We stay in the dark places of life by choice. We either like the dark or haven't stubbed our toes enough trying to walk in the dark yet to be sick of it. If you stay in the dark long enough and deal with the uncertainty of it, at some point, then you will flip the switch, call on His name, and let the light shine in.

Also, in the beginning, God brought light where darkness was. In the dark, there was nothing but chaos. I want to suggest that we are living in a season of chaos and confusion. In this season of chaos, police officers get off free for murdering an innocent woman sleeping in her bed; in this season of chaos where "I can't breathe" is a signal to put more weight on our necks; in this season of chaos, where a president pays less taxes in two years than a low-income person pays in a year; in this season of chaos where a virus is killing people without warning—in the current context of chaos, there is but one way for us to make it through: we have to flip the switch and turn on the light. His light is the only thing that can help the darkness of our rage and confusion. His light is the only thing that can help the darkness of our despair. There is only one difference between my light analogy and Christological reality. Light bulbs run out after shining for so long. After a while, you have to change the light. But not so with Jesus. What He did on the Cross of Calvary seals the reality that His light never dims. His light never goes out. I can call on Him without a quota. He will step in, no matter how many times I call.

In verse 13, the leaders complain that Jesus is praising Himself and doesn't adhere to the basic premise of the Jewish legal procedure of having a minimum of two or three witnesses. But that's because they were still in the darkness and had no vision. If they flipped the switch, then they would know that He had every witness resident within Himself. He need not check with anyone. Every witness He needs is wrapped up with God IN THREE PERSONS. Aren't you glad that Jesus does not need to check with anyone outside of Himself before doing anything in your life? So, my suggestion to you is to *walk in the light, beautiful light; come where the dewdrops of mercy shine bright. Shine all around us by day and by night: Jesus, the light of the world.*

THE GREAT HYMN
SHINE ON ME

I heard the voice of Jesus say,
"Come unto me and rest.
Lay down thou weary one, lay down
Thy head upon my breast."

Shine on me, Shine on me.
Let the light from the lighthouse,
Shine on me.
Shine on me. Shine on me.
Let the light from the lighthouse
shine on me.

With pitying eyes the Prince of Peace
Beheld our helpless grief;
He saw, and O amazing love!
He came to our relief. [Refrain]

PASTOR BREONUS M. MITCHELL SR.
Mount Gilead Missionary Baptist Church
Nashville, Tennessee

PASTOR BREONUS M. MITCHELL SR.
MOUNT GILEAD MISSIONARY BAPTIST CHURCH
NASHVILLE, TENNESSEE

JESUS IS GOD

John 10:22-30

22 And it was at Jerusalem the feast of the dedication, and it was winter.

23 And Jesus walked in the temple in Solomon's porch.

24 Then came the Jews round about him, and said unto him, How long dost thou make us to doubt? If thou be the Christ, tell us plainly.

25 Jesus answered them, I told you, and ye believed not: the works that I do in my Father's name, they bear witness of me.

26 But ye believe not, because ye are not of my sheep, as I said unto you.

27 My sheep hear my voice, and I know them, and they follow me:

28 And I give unto them eternal life; and they shall never perish, neither shall any man pluck them out of my hand.

29 My Father, which gave them me, is greater than all; and no man is able to pluck them out of my Father's hand.

30 I and my Father are one.

THE GREAT HYMN
TO GOD BE THE GLORY

How can I say thanks
for the things you have done for me
Things so undeserved
Yet you give to prove your love for me
The voices of a million angels
Could not express my gratitude
All that I am and ever hope to be
I owe it all to Thee

To God be the glory
To God be the glory
To God be the glory
For the things He has done
With His blood, He has saved me
With His power, He has raised me.
To God be the glory
For the things he has done

Just let me live my life
Let it be pleasing, Lord to Thee
Should I gain any praise,
Let it go to Calvary.

With His blood, He has saved me
With His power, He has raised me.
To God be the glory
For the things he has done.

Lord, Your enduring mystery causes me to know that You are indeed God. Thank You for becoming one of us to save us from ourselves. I bless Your name for paying a debt that You did not owe because we had a debt that we could not pay. God, thank You so much for becoming one of the sons of men so that sons of men might become sons of God. The petition I lay before You in this prayer is this: take the mercy of the moment and the mystery of Your deity and cause revival the world over as people genuinely discover who You are and what You accomplished for us at the Cross. In the name of Jesus I pray. Amen.

Article 15

**THE GREAT HIM
JESUS IS GOD
John 10:22-30**

**by
Pastor Breonus M. Mitchell Sr.**

There is an adage that goes, "Be careful of what you do around your children." The wisdom and warnings are simple: children model what they see in their parents and not what they hear. Such is the case with my youngest son, Brennon. He seems to imitate and mimic, replicate and reproduce everything that I do. Not so long ago, we had his first eye examination. What was unusual and uncommon was his enthusiasm and eagerness about the appointment. Although I made it clear he might not need glasses, in the days leading to the examination, he made it clear that he anticipated and awaited having to wear glasses. To Brennon's pleasure and not my own, he would need glasses—as virtual learning has affected his vision. With a selection of frames before him, Brennon chooses a frame that is the color and style of frames I recently purchased following my eye examination. Of course, I inquired and asked why. He responded, answering, "I want to look like you." Brennon, again, seems to imitate, mimic, replicate, and reproduce everything that I do.

Such is the case that we are presented within John 10:22-31. Jesus, answering the inquiry and inquisition of the Jews regarding His identity as the Messiah, says, "The works that I do in my father's name, they bear witness of me. . . . I and my Father are one" (verses 25, 30). What does this statement suggest? What is its claim? The claim of this statement is this: to hear and see the Son is to hear and see the Father.

The gospel of John is the most theological of the quartet of canonical Gospel writings. He writes to make known that Jesus is the Godman. This is obvious and observable in its introduction. He wastes no time with tracing the human genealogy of Jesus. He makes no effort to bring Christ through forty-two generations. No. John is a theologian. So, he writes this: "In the beginning was the Word, and the Word was with God, and the Word was God. He was in the beginning with God. All things were made through him, and without him was not any thing made that was made. In him was life, and the life was the light of men. The light shines in the darkness, and the darkness has not overcome it" (John 1:1-5, ESV).

The fourth Gospel is emphatic that the one who sent Jesus into the world is the Father and that Jesus is His Son. Jesus, however, does not come into the world to reveal that God is like a Father—something new from Israel's Scriptures—but to reveal that God is His Father apart from whom Jesus is/can do nothing. Consequently, to hear and see the Son is to hear and see the Father.

Within the Johannine gospel's theological world, there is no access to God apart from the revelation of the Son. Oneness! Perhaps this is among the most cloudy, complicated, and confusing claims of our Lord, Jesus Christ. But what does it mean or how are we to interpret the words of Christ—when He emphatically and unequivocally affirms, "I and the Father are one"?

"Christology and theology are so intimately related in the Fourth Gospel," Frank Matera writes, "that it is impossible to discuss the Son without speaking of the Father, just as it is impossible to discuss the Father without speaking of the Son." He continues, "Since the Son is the light of the world who comes to reveal what he has seen and heard in the presence of the Father, the true situation of the world can only be known in light of the revelation the Son brings from the Father." This, then, is the claim of this statement. Again, to hear and see the Son is to hear and see the Father.

In the context of this chapter, the parallelism between what Jesus says of Himself in verse 28b and of God in verse 29b (the sheep are secure in the hands of each) underscores the fact that Jesus and God do the same work; what is true of the work of one is true of the work of the other. Therefore, what is critical here is that we read verse 30 in the context of Johannine theology and not through the lens of the Christological controversies of the second through fourth centuries or of the trinitarian doctrine that developed out of those controversies. The Greek word *one* (ἕν *hen*) is neuter, not masculine—so that Jesus is not saying that He and God are one person, nor even of one nature or essence. Instead, He is saying that He and God are *united* in the work that They do. It is impossible to distinguish Jesus' work from God's work, because Jesus shares fully in God's work. The *prima facie* meaning of "I and the Father are one" in its Johannine context may well be the functional one that Father and Son work in perfect unity. Again, to hear and see the Son is to hear and see the Father.

In closing, the words of our risen Redeemer remind us of the mutual indwelling of the Trinity. Through the example of Jesus, they challenge us to become full participants in the work of

God. These words remind us that we have been called to finish what Jesus started. These words remind us that there are yet souls to save. These words remind us that there are yet lives to be changed.

So . . .
Work, for the night is coming,
Work thru the morning hours;
Work while the dew is sparkling,
Work 'mid springing flow'rs.
Work when the day grows brighter,
Work in the glowing sun;
Work, for the night is coming,
When man's work is done.
Work, for the night is coming,
Work thru the sunny noon;
Fill brightest hours with labor—
Rest comes, sure and soon.
Give ev'ry flying minute
Something to keep in-store;
Work, for the night is coming,
When man works no more.

Work, for the night is coming,
Under the sunset skies;
While their bright tints are glowing,
Work, for daylight flies.
Work till the last beam fadeth,
Fadeth to shine no more;
Work, while the night is dark'ning,
When man's work is o'er.

THE GREAT HYMN
MUST JESUS BEAR THE CROSS ALONE

Must Jesus bear this cross alone
And all this world go free?
There's the cross for everyone
And the the cross for me

Amazing grace, how sweet, how sweet it all sounds
I know, You saved, You saved the rich like me
Then I was once lost but know I now that I'm found
I was blind but now I know that I can see

Not alone, not alone, not alone
No Jesus cannot bear this cross alone
There's the cross for everyone and the cross for me

I came to my Jesus just as, just as I was
I was weary, I was wounded and sad
But I know that I found in Him a resting, a resting place
And now, right now my heart, my heart feel bad, oh, Lord

Not alone, not alone, not alone
No, not alone, oh, Jesus, not alone
No not alone, I know, the world go free
There's the cross for everyone and I know, the cross for me

DR. F. BERNARD MITCHELL
Zion Hill Baptist Church
Mendenhall, Mississippi

DR. F. BERNARD MITCHELL
ZION HILL BAPTIST CHURCH
MENDENHALL, MISSISSIPPI

JESUS IS OUR RISEN LORD

1 Corinthians 15:1-8

1 Moreover, brethren, I declare unto you the gospel which I preached unto you, which also ye have received, and wherein ye stand;

2 By which also ye are saved, if ye keep in memory what I preached unto you, unless ye have believed in vain.

3 For I delivered unto you first of all that which I also received, how that Christ died for our sins according to the scriptures;

4 And that he was buried, and that he rose again the third day according to the scriptures:

5 And that he was seen of Cephas, then of the twelve:

6 After that, he was seen of above five hundred brethren at once; of whom the greater part remain unto this present, but some are fallen asleep.

7 After that, he was seen of James; then of all the apostles.

8 And last of all he was seen of me also, as of one born out of due time.

THE GREAT HYMN
CHRIST THE RISEN LORD TODAY

Christ the Lord is ris'n today, Alleluia!
Sons of men and angels say, Alleluia!
Raise your joys and triumphs high, Alleluia!
Sing, ye heav'ns, and earth, reply, Alleluia!
Lives again our glorious King, Alleluia!

⊠Where, O death, is now thy sting? Alleluia!
Once He died our souls to save, Alleluia!
Where thy victory, O grave? Alleluia!
Love's redeeming work is done, Alleluia!
Fought the fight, the battle won, Alleluia!

Death in vain forbids His rise, Alleluia!
Christ hath opened paradise, Alleluia!
Soar we now where Christ hath led, Alleluia!
Foll'wing our exalted Head, Alleluia!

Made like Him, like Him we rise, Alleluia!
Ours the cross, the grave, the skies, Alleluia!
Hail the Lord of earth and heaven, Alleluia!
Praise to Thee by both be given, Alleluia!

Thee we greet triumphant now, Alleluia!
Hail the Resurrection, thou, Alleluia!
King of glory, Soul of bliss, Alleluia!
Everlasting life is this, Alleluia!
Thee to know, Thy pow'r to prove, Alleluia!
Thus to sing, and thus to love, Alleluia!

Lord of Calvary, thank You for being our risen Lord. To know that You have suffered, bled, died, and risen makes life worth living every day. My reflections of the Cross make me understand that the debt that I owe You can never be repaid. Please, I pray, receive this praise—my soul cries "Thank You" for what You have done for me. My sacred supplication before Your throne at this moment is this: as You rose from the dead after being crucified on the skull, rise, and reign in every heart that has come to know You—and reach those who have not come to know You with Your redemptive love that will change their lives forever. In Jesus' name I pray. Amen.

Article 16

THE GREAT HIM
JESUS IS OUR RISEN LORD
1 Corinthians 15:1-8

by
Dr. F. Bernard Mitchell

The torture of Calvary is now over. The horror from the hill called Golgotha is finished. The Scripture has now been fulfilled. The sacrificial Lamb has been slain. The body has been begged for and buried before the beginning of the Sabbath. He has lain in the grave but now it's Sunday morning. It's time for my sacrifice to become my Savior. It is time for Him to have risen from the dead. The evidence of His resurrection is our belief. Christians have all the proof they need in the Word of God. Paul writes to this Corinthian church to give them insight into the Resurrection. Paul is teaching the church at Corinth that belief is not based on a visual witness; it is based upon the communication of the story and one's own belief. We should not have to prove that He has risen. I don't need visual evidence. I don't have to fly to the Holy Land, go to the grave, and see that it is empty. I know He has risen because I heard the story communicated to me by the preaching of the Gospel—that Jesus died but rose again. Paul shows that the foundation of the Bible is that Jesus died on a cross, was buried in a grave, and was resurrected from the dead.

The Risen Lord teaches me that one can't rise without assistance. Paul continually clarifies that Jesus didn't get Himself up, but God raised Him from the dead. The resurrection in your life is not an independent act. The same God that raised Jesus is the same God that can raise you. He has Lordship because of His resurrection. He has the authority to help me in any capacity I may need. He showed the man in Him when He died on the Cross and the God in Him when He was raised from the dead. There are many ways he assisted in the Resurrection, but I will give just one: There was a stone in front of the grave. It was blocking the exit and entrance to the grave. God removed that which was blocking Jesus from coming out of the grave. When He removed the blockage, Jesus was free to come out. God can remove your blockage. Then you are free to come out.

He shows me that there is no success without sacrifice. Crucifixion and resurrection are joined together. If there were no crucifixion, then there would not have been a resurrection. Your sacrifice is a part of the process for your success. No one likes suffering, but it's part of the process to success. When we watch Jesus struggle, we see His determination, His love for man, and His obedience to God. He arose stronger. We knew before Calvary that He had power. He had the ability to heal the sick, give sight to the blind, stop blood flows, unstop deaf ears, make the lame walk, raise people from the dead, cleanse lepers, turn water into wine, calm the water, and walk on water. He has power, but now He has all power. The Resurrection gave Him all authority. He is my risen Lord, because He's the only being in my life that has all power. I do not have to look for another source. I do not have to find other assistance. Whatever I need, Jesus has it. If only you believe that Jesus is our risen Lord, you have access to whatever you need. The most significant part is that my connection with Christ gives a guarantee to eternal life. Christ has prepared a place for me to dwell with Him—the place where I will spend eternity. The truth is that I'm not worthy of being there, but because of the sacrifice of Jesus, I have entrance. If someone asks me how I got in, I will tell him/her, "I'm with Him"—the one who died, was buried, and rose from the dead. I'm with Him, the one that rules heaven and earth. I'm with Him, the one that speaks and creation obeys. I'm with Him, the one that saved my soul. He is my risen Lord.

There was a man trying to get a job, but the problem was that he was being blocked from coming into the building. He submitted his application and résumé, and they were both accepted. The man he was to meet was the person that hired everyone in the corporation, and the building was heavily secured. When he received the appointment, he was also supposed to receive a pass to print out, but he did not receive it. When he arrived, security would not let him enter. He tried to explain that he had an appointment, but he didn't have a pass. The security guard told him that if he were to let him through, there would be another security point he would have to go through that would not allow him to gain entrance. The man was very distressed, standing outside of the building. A young man walked up and asked the man what was wrong. He explained that he had an appointment for a job he needed, but he couldn't get in because they hadn't e-mailed him the pass. The young man told him, "Just follow me in, and when they ask you where you are going just tell them, 'I'm with him.'" When they got to security, the officer said, "I told you that you can't enter without a pass." The man said, "I'm with him." He went through. When he arrived at the next checkpoint, they asked him for his pass. The man said, "I'm with him." He finally made it into the man's office, walking behind the young man. The man stood up and said, "Hello, Son, what's going on?" The Son said, "I have this man that needs a job." He said, "If my son brought you, then the job is yours." Our risen Lord, the Son of God, takes care of us.

THE GREAT HYMN
NOTHING BUT THE BLOOD

What can wash away my sin?
Nothing but the blood of Jesus;
What can make me whole again?
Nothing but the blood of Jesus.

Refrain: Oh! precious is the flow
That makes me white as snow;
No other fount I know,
Nothing but the blood of Jesus.

For my pardon, this I see,
Nothing but the blood of Jesus;
For my cleansing this my plea,
Nothing but the blood of Jesus.
Nothing can for sin atone,
Nothing but the blood of Jesus;
Naught of good that I have done,
Nothing but the blood of Jesus.

This is all my hope and peace,
Nothing but the blood of Jesus;
This is all my righteousness,
Nothing but the blood of Jesus.

Now by this I'll overcome—
Nothing but the blood of Jesus;
Now by this I'll reach my home—
Nothing but the blood of Jesus.

Glory! Glory! This I sing—
Nothing but the blood of Jesus,
All my praise for this I bring—
Nothing but the blood of Jesus.

PASTOR TOLAN J. MORGAN
Fellowship Bible Baptist Church
Warner Robins, Georgia

PASTOR TOLAN J. MORGAN
FELLOWSHIP BIBLE BAPTIST CHURCH
WARNER ROBINS, GEORGIA

JESUS IS THE TRUE VINE

John 15:1-7

1 I am the true vine, and my Father is the husbandman.

2 Every branch in me that beareth not fruit he taketh away: and every branch that beareth fruit, he purgeth it, that it may bring forth more fruit.

3 Now ye are clean through the word which I have spoken unto you.

4 Abide in me, and I in you. As the branch cannot bear fruit of itself, except it abide in the vine; no more can ye, except ye abide in me.

5 I am the vine, ye are the branches: He that abideth in me, and I in him, the same bringeth forth much fruit: for without me ye can do nothing.

6 If a man abide not in me, he is cast forth as a branch, and is withered; and men gather them, and cast them into the fire, and they are burned.

7 If ye abide in me, and my words abide in you, ye shall ask what ye will, and it shall be done unto you.

THE GREAT HYMN
ABIDE IN THE VINE

We've found the secret of living,
We've seen the vision divine:
We are of God in Christ Jesus,
We're abiding, abiding in the vine.
Abiding in the vine,
Abiding in the vine,
All the riches of God's life are mine!
Praise God, He put us here,
Never to leave; oh, we're—
Abiding, abiding in the vine.

No more in vain need we struggle,
Trying the way in to find.
Praise God—we're in Him already,
Hallelujah, abiding in the vine.

In us, the ointment is moving,
'Tis the anointing divine;
God's precious essence bestowing,
While abiding, abiding in the vine.

Now in the life-flow we're living,
O how the light in us shines!
Both God and man are at home now
By the mutual abiding in the vine.

Eternal God, our Father, I pause at this moment to thank You for the path You have designed for us to be reconciled to You. Keep us near You as a vinedresser cares for a precious vine that he knows will bring forth fruit. O God, cause those who believe to prosper and increase just as a well-kept vine produces its fruit in the right season. In the name that is above every name—the name Jesus—I pray. Amen.

Article 17

THE GREAT HIM
JESUS IS THE TRUE VINE
John 15:1-7

by
Pastor Tolan J. Morgan

Our Lord Jesus Christ was the Master of using everyday, natural elements as reference points to reveal profound, spiritual truths about Himself and His kingdom. We are placing focus now on one such example where Jesus said, "I am the true vine, and my Father is the husbandman." This statement was the last of the notable I AM declarations of Christ tucked away in John's biography of Jesus. These I AM declarations were exclusive to John's writings because they supported his thesis that Jesus was God, and they made a direct correlation of Christ to the Name by which God introduced Himself to Moses in Exodus 3:14. In particular, this declaration summoned the senses and invited the intellect of His disciples to explore the exposition of a vine as a symbolic vehicle of His own Self-disclosure. Shall we then consider several significant revelations associated therewith?

Christ wanted the disciples (along with us) to receive the revelation through the vine that He was the Perfect Fulfillment to an imperfect history. There were instances in the Old Testament's prophetic literature where Israel was represented figuratively as a vine. Isaiah wrote, "What could have been done more to my vineyard, that I have not done in it? wherefore, when I looked that it should bring forth grapes, brought it forth wild grapes?" (Isaiah 5:4). Jeremiah added, "Yet I had planted thee a noble vine, wholly a right seed: how then art thou turned into the degenerate plant of a strange vine unto me?" (Jeremiah 2:21). Hosea raised this indictment that "Israel is an empty vine, he bringeth forth fruit unto himself: according to the multitude of his fruit he hath increased the altars; according to the goodness of his land they have made goodly images" (Hosea 10:1). We see consistency with these prophets in pitching God as the establisher and owner of a vineyard in which He planted the vine named Israel.

Unfortunately, they had become contaminated, imperfect, and subsequently fraudulent in their function to produce for God due to their idolatry. However, Jesus revealed that He was the true vine. He purported that He was the complete, perfect version of that incomplete, imperfect vine that preceded Him. This is confirmed in His referring to Himself as the vine that is true. That word *true* is transliterated "alethinos" from the Greek New Testament text, and it "denotes the sense of real, ideal, or genuine." In this context, He Jesus was not contrasting Himself with something false. He was not the true light or the true vine than the untrue, but true as answering to the perfect ideal, and as opposed to all more or less imperfect representations. He was ideally true. Ideal truth, of which the natural vine is a figure, was fulfilled in Him. The application here juxtaposes something incomplete against something that is fulfilled and accomplished. Both Christ and Israel were vines of God. Both shared a natural mutuality from the human perspective. However, Christ was communicating that He was the present fulfillment to a historically incomplete and imperfect people.

Jesus used the vine to communicate another significant revelation about Himself—in that He was the Perfect Mediator for an imperfect relationship. In the pericope of John 15:1-8, Jesus made this declaration in relation to the husbandman and the branches. In John 15:1, His Father was the husbandman. The word *husbandman* is transliterated "georgos" from the Greek New Testament text, and it means "land-worker, farmer, a tiller of the ground, vinedresser."

In John 15:5, His disciples were the branches. So, as Jesus described Himself as the true vine, He was the mediator or the middleman that brought definition to how both parties interacted with Him as well as with each other. In summation, the branches drew their vitality and fruitfulness from remaining and abiding in the vine according to John 15:5. On the other hand, the husbandman received glorification for the branches' fruitfulness that resulted from their abiding in the vine. Therefore, Jesus was communicating through this vine metaphor that He was a necessity for both parties because He brought glory to the husbandman and growth to the branches. Simply put: He brought praise to the one and productivity to the other. Christ brought meaning to both parties, but He also brought mediation between both parties. He stood and continues to stand as the mediator between the Perfect and the imperfect to do one thing: bring them together. His goal was not to achieve a truce but to achieve reconciliation and the restoration of a healthy, holy relationship between God and humanity.

May we observe the following: John 15:4 indicates that the branches' ability to produce fruit was not of themselves, but their productivity (or lack thereof) was contingent on their wherewithal to abide in the vine. This is because the branches received life and productivity from the relationship the vine had with the husbandman. This observation now spotlights a doctrinal truth that salvation is not a covenant between God and man. On the contrary, salvation is a covenant between God and Jesus. In eternity past, the Father, Son, and Spirit voluntarily and freely chose the roles they would take in bringing about the redemption of God's people. This is what is called the Eternal Covenant of Redemption. The Father chose to be the fount and source of the entirety of the work; the Son chose to be the Redeemer and to enter into human flesh as one subject to the Father; and the Spirit chose to be Sanctifier of the church, the indwelling Testifier of Jesus Christ. In this covenant, humanity is the beneficiary and not a constituent.

Just as the vine is the go-between for the husbandman and the branches, so Jesus is the mediator between God and humanity. Jesus chose to bear the wrath of God for the sins of humanity in order that humanity may be reconciled back to God. The idea is not mere cancellation of sin, which could be arbitrary forgiveness based on a whim. Rather, judgment is averted because Christ took the punishment in our place—intentional substitution stressed by both Old and New Testaments. Hence, Jesus communicated through this vine metaphor that He was the Perfect Mediator who brought appeasement to the One and atonement to the other so that they could be reunited together again.

Third, Jesus used this vine metaphor to reveal Himself as the Perfect Source for Perpetual Productivity. This revelation is specific to the branches. Jesus stated in John 15:2-6 that the degree of productivity from the branches determines whether the branches are taken away, purged, or cast away (in that order). If a branch is unproductive, the husbandman takes it away. This does not mean he detaches it from the vine so soon. However, the phrase "takes away" is transliterated *airo* from the Greek New Testament text, and it means "to lift or raise."

This is the picture of a farmer who wraps certain plants' vines around a stick to keep the produce from being overcome by dirt that results from being too low to the ground. Thus, the farmer gives the branch another chance to be productive by repositioning it. Once it starts to produce fruit, the husbandman can opt to purge it by cutting away excess growth of other things that are not its intended fruit. He cuts away that excess growth because it occupies space needed for more intended fruit to come forth. In essence, purging prepares the branches for greater productivity.

On the contrary, branches that do not bring forth fruit are unproductive because they do not abide in the vine; and the husbandman then has the right to cast them away to wither and be thrown into the fire. There are two theological truths suggested here. First, God extends justice before judgment. He gives us (the branches) every opportunity to be productive before finally executing His judgment. This is why He sent Jesus, for He took it upon Himself to provide a way of escaping His judgment. Second, Jesus revealed through this vine metaphor that He gives life to the branches, He supplies nutrients for their fruitfulness, and He is consequently the ultimate source of both cause and effect.

A common by-product of the fruit of the vine was wine. This point made this particular I AM declaration revelatory and timely, given the fact that Jesus declared He was the true vine just after He and His disciples had finished the Last Supper. Wine, then, would have been a visual prop on the table as He spoke, or it would have been a taste lingering on their palates. In either case, the disciples could make a quick and familiar association to the fruit of the vine and its effervescent effects. Throughout Scripture, wine was associated with joy and celebration. Here in this context, Jesus associated wine with His blood. Therefore, at Calvary, Jesus would be the vine hung on the wood to be crushed for the production of wine and subsequent restoration of joy that accompanies being in a reconciled relationship with God. It is here that we understand Jesus to be our Source for perpetual life, fruitfulness, and joy. In this vein, Jesus as the vine is the Son of the One and the Source of the other.

In conclusion, may we be fully convinced to accept and proclaim Jesus Christ as the ultimate revelation of God and the uncompromising necessity for humanity. He is the true vine that brings God and humanity together at the intersection of the Cross. He is the true vine that brings partnership, productivity, and peace to the two parties. As we have been invited to revisit John 15:1, may we be reminded of the repetitive and imperative call to abide in Him that we may experience and enjoy life in the Vine.

THE GREAT HYMN
IT IS WELL

When peace like a river, attendeth my way,
When sorrows like sea billows roll
Whatever my lot, thou hast taught me to say
It is well, it is well, with my soul
It is well
With my soul
It is well, it is well with my soul

Though Satan should buffet, though trials should come,
Let this blest assurance control,
That Christ has regarded my helpless estate,
And hath shed His own blood for my soul
It is well (it is well)
With my soul (with my soul)
It is well, it is well with my soul

My sin, oh, the bliss of this glorious thought
My sin, not in part but the whole,
Is nailed to the cross, and I bear it no more,
Praise the Lord, praise the Lord, o my soul

It is well (it is well)
With my soul (with my soul)
It is well, it is well with my soul
It is well (it is well)
With my soul (with my soul)
It is well, it is well with my soul

PASTOR SHARON Y. RILEY
Agape Perfecting Praise & Worship Center
Orlando, Florida

PASTOR SHARON Y. RILEY
AGAPE PERFECTING PRAISE & WORSHIP CENTER
ORLANDO, FLORIDA

JESUS IS THE VICTORIOUS ONE

Revelation 3:14-21

14 And unto the angel of the church of the Laodiceans write; These things saith the Amen, the faithful and true witness, the beginning of the creation of God;

15 I know thy works, that thou art neither cold nor hot: I would thou wert cold or hot.

16 So then because thou art lukewarm, and neither cold nor hot, I will spue thee out of my mouth.

17 Because thou sayest, I am rich, and increased with goods, and have need of nothing; and knowest not that thou art wretched, and miserable, and poor, and blind, and naked:

18 I counsel thee to buy of me gold tried in the fire, that thou mayest be rich; and white raiment, that thou mayest be clothed, and that the shame of thy nakedness do not appear; and anoint thine eyes with eyesalve, that thou mayest see.

19 As many as I love, I rebuke and chasten: be zealous therefore, and repent.

20 Behold, I stand at the door, and knock: if any man hear my voice, and open the door, I will come in to him, and will sup with him, and he with me.

21 To him that overcometh will I grant to sit with me in my throne, even as I also overcame, and am set down with my Father in his throne.

THE GREAT HYMN
VICTORY IN JESUS

I heard an old, old story, how a Savior came from glory
How He gave His life on Calvary to save a wretch like me
I heard about His groaning, of His precious blood's atoning
Then I repented of my sins and won the victory

Oh victory in Jesus, my Savior forever
He sought me and bought me with His redeeming blood
He loved me 'ere I knew Him and all my love is due Him
He plunged me to victory beneath the cleansing flood

I heard about His healing, of His cleansing power revealing
How He made the lame to walk again and
'caused the blind to see
And then I cried, "Dear Jesus, come and
heal my broken spirit"
And somehow Jesus came and brought to me the victory

Oh victory in Jesus, my Savior forever
He sought me and He bought me with His redeeming blood
He loved me 'ere I knew Him and all my love is due Him
He plunged me to victory beneath the cleansing flood, c'mon

Oh victory in Jesus, my Savior forever
He sought me and He bought me with His redeeming blood
He loved me 'ere I knew Him and all my love is due Him
He plunged me to victory beneath the cleansing flood
He plunged me to victory beneath the cleansing flood

Merciful Master, there are times when I feel defeated, dejected, and distressed when I consider some of the things with which I am confronted. However, just knowing that You have never had an enemy You could not defeat makes me cry Your praises in public places for all the world to see. Lord, I pray even now that defeat never again will have a place in my life as long as You are on the throne of my human existence. In Jesus' name I pray. Amen!

The HIM BOOK

Article 18

THE GREAT HIM
JESUS IS THE VICTORIOUS ONE
Revelation 3:14-21

by
Pastor Sharon Y. Riley

John Carlin's book *Playing the Enemy: Nelson Mandela and the Game That Made a Nation* details South African events surrounding the 1995 Rugby World Cup. The demise of apartheid in South Africa ushered in an unprecedented order that was met with much resistance and threats of defeat, but ultimately, victory. South Africa's national underdog rugby team, the Springboks, became the automatic entry into the World Cup as the nation hosted the competition. Apartheid, characterized by Afrikaans as "apartness," was an authoritarian political culture based on baasskap, or white supremacy. The culture subjugated South Africa's non-white majority and positioned South Africa's white minority at the helm of the nation's political, social, and economic systems. The book provided the storyline for the 2009 film adaptation, *Invictus*. The film portrays the true story of how South Africa's first black president, President Nelson Mandela, met with the predominantly black South African Sports Committee and partnered with the rugby team's captain, Francois Pienaar, a son of apartheid, to help unite their divided country. The Latin translation of "Invictus" is "undefeated, unsubdued, invincible, undisputed, or unconquered." In English, it translates as "victorious." While in prison, Mandela found inspiration in William Ernest Henley's poem "Invictus." The poem was written during Henley's three-year infirmary stay as he lay recovering from multiple procedures that left him with one leg to stand on by the age of 16. Henley was determined to prevail against the pain and defeat of the disability that left him maimed, yet masterful; hence the title "Invictus," or unconquered. Henley's inspiration postured Mandela to face adversity and not be overcome by it. During the 1995 Rugby World Cup, South Africa's Springboks personified the poem's title and made an undefeated run for a final finish as the World Cup Champions; they were victorious.

"The Apokalypsis," or the Revelation of Jesus Christ which God gave to Him, is the apostle John's transcription or testimony through divine vision of God's final victory over every evil force. "Conquering," winning the victory, is a key word in Revelation's Christology and an

143

essential idea in understanding the Believer's life. The one who conquers is the victor. Jesus "overcame"/"conquered" (Revelation 3:21, ESV) to secure a "conquering"/"overcoming" life for the Believer. Conquering implies imminent contests, battles, or contention in the life of the Believer and an assurance of inevitable victory secured by Jesus' triumph on the Cross. For the Believers who overcome as Jesus did, He promises the highest attainable honor, a "ruling position in the messianic kingdom."

Jesus Christ, the Victorious One, has waged war against Satan, making it possible for faithful Believers to do God's work, keep God's Word, and share in the victory that Jesus has already won by laying down His life. Because of Jesus' sacrifice and victory over sin and death, the faithful Believer is able to overcome trouble and tribulation in a toxic world. What appeared to be Jesus' defeat and demise at Calvary translated into victory, once and for all. Jesus laid down His life willingly according to John 10:18—"No man taketh it from me, but I lay it down of myself. I have power to lay it down, and I have power to take it again. This commandment have I received of my Father." The power and authority given to Jesus by God is exercised in the self-prediction of Jesus' death, and also in the actualization of Jesus' revival or resurrection. Victory is a summation of the fulfillment of Jesus' earthly mission. He overcame Satan, sin, death, darkness, and disease. He overcame the world. Jesus said in John 16:33b, "In the world ye shall have tribulation: but be of good cheer; I have overcome the world." The Overcomer overthrew every system and struggle that conflicted with His mission to reveal God and expose human depravity. The word *overcome* is derived from the Greek word *nikao*, meaning "to conquer, carry off the victory, or come off victorious."

John's apocalyptic epistle to the seven churches in the Roman province of Asia predicts the ultimate triumph of the kingdom of God. In the conclusion of his letter to the Church at Laodicea, John draws out the stark contrast between this church and the others. The churches at Ephesus, Smyrna, Pergamum, Thyatira, Sardis, and Philadelphia all receive commendation and critique. However, the church at Laodicea is the one church that draws only rebuke. Laodicea was a banking and manufacturing epicenter, also known for its medical school. It was materially prosperous but spiritually bankrupt! The strong rebuke came in response to the self-righteous, self-reliant, and self-satisfied disposition of the church. Deceived by their wealth and wanting for nothing, the Laodicean church was charged with ineffectiveness as they lacked zeal and concern for others. John records the church's diagnosis as lukewarm, neither hot enough to heal nor cold enough to refresh.

Laodicea's geographic location positioned the city to receive a warm, sulphurous water supply—a striking contrast to the hot, medicinal waters of Hierapolis and the cold, pure springs of Colossae. Jesus' disgust with the climate of Laodicea flowed through the tip of John's pen when he wrote, "So then because thou art lukewarm, and neither cold nor hot, I will spue thee out of my mouth" in Revelation 3:16. However, His capacity to love the faithful and the foolish makes provision for the deliverance of the deficient. "For whom the LORD loveth he correcteth; even as a father the son in whom he delighteth" (Proverbs 3:12). In hostility, Jesus Christ (the Victorious One) opposes His enemies—but in humility, He draws the broken Laodicean church to Himself, appealing to anyone who will hear His voice. He doesn't barrage the church like law enforcement executing a no-knock warrant; instead, He presents Himself to the broken, creating an opportunity for repentance. To the individual overcomer who hears Jesus' voice, endures to the end, obeys His Word, and overcomes even as Christ overcame, he will receive a victor's reward. Jesus Christ, the Victorious One, has given overcoming power to every faithful Believer, "And they overcame him by the blood of the Lamb, and by the word of their testimony; and they loved not their lives unto the death" (Revelation 12:11).

Works Cited

Beale, G. K. *The Book of Revelation: A Commentary on the Greek Text.* Grand Rapids, MI: Paternoster Press, 1911.

Blue Letter Bible, "Gospel of John 16 – KJV- King James Version." Blue Letter Bible. 1996-2020. http://www.blbclassic.org/Bible.cfm?b=Jhn&c=16&t=KJV (accessed September 12, 2020).

Boring, M. E. *Revelation.* Louisville, KY: John Knox Press, 1989.

Harrington, Wilfrid J. *Revelation*—Sacra Pagina Series. Collegeville, MN: Liturgical Press, 2008.

Invictus (film), https://en.wikipedia.org/wiki/Invictus_(film) (accessed July 29, 2020).

"William Ernest Henley," *Encyclopaedia Britannica*, Inc.: August 19, 2020, https://www.britannica.com/biography/William-Ernest-Henley (accessed September 12, 2020).

THE GREAT HYMN
I AM THE VINE

I am the Vine, you are the branches
He who abides in Me and I in him
He it is that bears much fruit
For apart from Me you can do nothing (repeat)
If you abide in Me and My words abide in you
Ask what you will and it shall be given to you
I am the Vine, you are the branches
He who abides in Me and I in him
He it is that bears much fruit
For apart from Me you can do nothing

He it is that bears much fruit
For apart from Me you can do nothing

DR. JOHN R. ADOLPH
Antioch Missionary Baptist Church
Beaumont, Texas

DR. JOHN R. ADOLPH
ANTIOCH MISSIONARY BAPTIST CHURCH
BEAUMONT, TEXAS

JESUS IS LORD AND GOD

John 20:23-31

23 Whose soever sins ye remit, they are remitted unto them; and whose soever sins ye retain, they are retained.

24 But Thomas, one of the twelve, called Didymus, was not with them when Jesus came.

25 The other disciples therefore said unto him, We have seen the LORD. But he said unto them, Except I shall see in his hands the print of the nails, and put my finger into the print of the nails, and thrust my hand into his side, I will not believe.

26 And after eight days again his disciples were within, and Thomas with them: then came Jesus, the doors being shut, and stood in the midst, and said, Peace be unto you.

27 Then saith he to Thomas, Reach hither thy finger, and behold my hands; and reach hither thy hand, and thrust it into my side: and be not faithless, but believing.

28 And Thomas answered and said unto him, My LORD and my God.

29 Jesus saith unto him, Thomas, because thou hast seen me, thou hast believed: blessed are they that have not seen, and yet have believed.

30 And many other signs truly did Jesus in the presence of his disciples, which are not written in this book:

31 But these are written, that ye might believe that Jesus is the Christ, the Son of God; and that believing ye might have life through his name.

THE GREAT HYMN
CHRIST ALONE IS ENOUGH

Christ is my reward
And all of my devotion
Now there's nothing in this world
That could ever satisfy

Through every trial
My soul will sing
No turning back
I've been set free

Christ is enough for me
Christ is enough for me
Everything I need is in You
Everything I need

Christ my all in all
The joy of my salvation
And this hope will never fail
Heaven is our home

Through every storm
My soul will sing
Jesus is here
To God be the glory

Eternal God, I bow to honor You as the one true celebrity of the universe. There are none like You in heaven, on earth, or in hell. You are the Godman—the perfect redemptive union of humanity and divinity sent to save us from our sins. Thank You, O Lord, for Your saving power, and bless You, O God, for what took place on Calvary. In the name of Jesus I pray. Amen.

Article 19

**THE GREAT HIM
JESUS IS LORD AND GOD
John 20:23-31**

**by
Dr. John R. Adolph**

Dr. Leon Morris, a New Testament scholar and commentary writer, suggests the following regarding the person of Jesus Christ: "If we can offer no other certainties after reading the Gospel, according to John, we must conclude that Jesus is Lord." Dr. Cleopatrick Lacy, professor of Sermon Preparation and Delivery, makes a similar claim when he emphatically argues that "if Jesus Christ is not God He is the greatest counterfeit time has ever seen."

The bitter chill of a rather icy winter was slowly passing, and things in the Olympic city of Atlanta started to heat up a bit. I was enrolled in twenty-one graduate study hours at the I.T.C. Morehouse School of Religion, and the light at the end of the tunnel reminded me that graduation was near. One of my classes turned out to be a rather hot-handled course often filled with debate, heated discussion, and sometimes downright debacle. It was Dr. Kenneth Henry's African American Church History course. Dr. Henry always presented a well-manicured lecture; the problem was that somehow the class participants would drift from his lecture into other heated subjects that would spark debate. On one occasion, for a devotional reading in class, a young lady read John 20:26-29, in which the disciple Thomas called Jesus "my LORD and my God" (John 20:28). As soon as the student closed the Bible and took her seat, the comments and queries commenced and never seemed to conclude. However, the one question that loomed about that no one wanted to address was this: "What does it mean for Jesus to be Lord and God?"

The core, crux, and center of this article rest within the confines of this one question. The answer to this one query separates blessing from cursing, unbelievers from believers, sinners from saints, citizens of heaven from sinners trapped eternally in hell. Undoubtedly, the disciple Thomas had seen Jesus before. However, what did he encounter this time to make him speak of Jesus in such glorious terms? What did Thomas mean when he uttered the words, "my Lord and my God"? This article will briefly analyze the root meaning of *Lord* and *God* as used in the passage.

"Jesus is Lord" means that He has been resurrected. When Thomas looks at Jesus, he does not see a walking corpse but, rather, a living Christ. Jesus invites Thomas to touch His wounded hands and side. However, the most amazing facet of the Resurrection is not the fact that death could not hold Jesus; neither could the grave contain Him. The most amazing fact is that the wounds from the Cross are still present. More specifically, Jesus has piercing wounds in five places on His body: both hands, both feet, and His side. What do these marks mean as it relates to His being resurrected? These marks are proof of purchase. The redemption of humankind came with a price tag attached. They prove that redemption cost Jesus His life; however, the Redeemer that was dead has now been resurrected.

A closer look at the passage reveals the fact that "Jesus is Lord" means that He rules. The word choice used in the pericope for "Lord" comes from the Koine Greek term *Kurios*; it means "to possess authority." It is interesting to note that the reality of authority comes with boundaries and jurisdictions. More illustratively put, a state trooper from Texas cannot give you a speeding ticket in New York because he is out of his jurisdiction. However, when the name *Jesus* rises to the surface, His ability to rule has no boundary, His jurisdiction has no limit, and His authority has no match or parallel. He does not have an assistant Lord or a counsel of lords that governs with Him. He alone is Lord. He rules, and He super rules. There is no other rule besides His. Jesus Himself put it on this order after His resurrection from the grave. He said, "All power is given unto me in heaven and in earth" (Matthew 28:18). Again, "Jesus is Lord" means that He rules.

Most importantly, "Jesus is Lord" means that He is remarkably unique. Thomas looks at Jesus and declares that He is "my Lord and my God." As mentioned earlier, the term *Lord* means "to possess authority." Notice, however, that the term *Lord* is now attached to the term *God* (*Theos*). The blessing of this segment of the passage is found in the grammatical application of the word *and*, which is being used as a descriptive conjunction. With this in mind, the text should be translated like this: "my Lord, who is my God." With this in mind, to be Lord means to be God. There is a divinely necessitated redemptive requirement that mandates that Jesus be both human and divine simultaneously. This necessary facet is found in the fact that the only one who could meet God's righteous requirement to pay the debt owed for sin would be God Himself. Thus, the only way to redeem a thing is to become the thing you seek to redeem. God became us to save us, and He did it in the person of Jesus Christ.

So, the class wrestled in a debate-like fashion with the issue of what it meant for Jesus to be Lord and God when, all of a sudden, a student from Michigan just leaped into the conversation without raising his hand and said it best; he said, "There are none like Him—in heaven, on earth, or in hell. Jesus Christ stands in a category all by Himself. He is human enough to become one of us, but God enough to save us from our sins. He is Lord because He is God! He is seated at the right hand of the Father on high and shall reign forever and ever and ever!"

THE GREAT HYMN
HE IS LORD, HE IS LORD

He is Lord, He is Lord
He has risen from the dead
And He is Lord – 2
Every knee shall bow
Every tongue confess
That Jesus Christ is Lord

You are Lord, You are Lord
You have risen from the dead
And You are Lord
Every knee shall bow
Every tongue confess
That Jesus Christ is Lord

DR. GINA M. STEWART
Christ Missionary Baptist Church
Memphis, Tennessee

DR. GINA M. STEWART
CHRIST MISSIONARY BAPTIST CHURCH
MEMPHIS, TENNESSEE

JESUS IS ALPHA AND OMEGA

Revelation 1:1-8

1 The Revelation of Jesus Christ, which God gave unto him, to shew unto his servants things which must shortly come to pass; and he sent and signified it by his angel unto his servant John:

2 Who bare record of the word of God, and of the testimony of Jesus Christ, and of all things that he saw.

3 Blessed is he that readeth, and they that hear the words of this prophecy, and keep those things which are written therein: for the time is at hand.

4 John to the seven churches which are in Asia: Grace be unto you, and peace, from him which is, and which was, and which is to come; and from the seven Spirits which are before his throne;

5 And from Jesus Christ, who is the faithful witness, and the first begotten of the dead, and the prince of the kings of the earth. Unto him that loved us, and washed us from our sins in his own blood,

6 And hath made us kings and priests unto God and his Father; to him be glory and dominion for ever and ever. Amen.

7 Behold, he cometh with clouds; and every eye shall see him, and they also which pierced him: and all kindreds of the earth shall wail because of him. Even so, Amen.

8 I am Alpha and Omega, the beginning and the ending, saith the Lord, which is, and which was, and which is to come, the Almighty.

THE GREAT HYMN
YOU ARE ALPHA AND OMEGA

You are Alpha and Omega, sing
We worship You our Lord
You are worthy to be praised
Sing it again

You are Alpha and Omega
We worship You our Lord
You are worthy to be praised
We give You all the glory
We worship You our Lord

You are worthy to be praised
We give You all the glory
(And we worship You)
We worship You our Lord

You are worthy to be praised
You are Alpha and Omega
We worship You our Lord
You are worthy to be praised

We give You all
We give You all
We give You all
We give You all the glory

We worship You our Lord
You are worthy to be praised
We give You all the glory
We worship You our Lord
You are worthy to be praised

Lord, to know that You were before the beginning and comprehend that You will be present when the end rolls up like words written on a scroll causes my soul to shout, "Only You, Jesus, only You!" God, as this petition is lifted before Your throne, glory is due You because You are the uncreated creator, the unmoved mover, and the unbegun beginning of all of that we see and encounter. Bless You for being our Alpha and Omega. Thank You for being everything in between. Now, Lord, hear this personal plea: order my steps in such a way that the conclusion of my life in time meets Your expectation that You had in mind when You created me. In the name of Jesus I pray. Amen!

Article 20

THE GREAT HIM
JESUS IS ALPHA AND OMEGA
Revelation 1:1-8

by
Dr. Gina M. Stewart

The book of Revelation is possibly one of the most challenging books of the Bible to read and comprehend. It is a kaleidoscope of strange visions, symbolic creatures, and prophecies that seem mysterious and quite alarming for some. Its message has often been obscured because of its violent language, vivid imagery, and bizarre-sounding content. Scholars, theologians, and pastors have often debated about ways to interpret it, while others have left its interpretation in the hands of overly zealous sensationalizers.

Thomas G. Long, the Bandy Professor of Preaching Emeritus at Candler School of Theology at Emory University, has described the book as a literary hybrid. Long asserts that on the one hand, it is an apocalypse, a literary form in which the author speaks in visionary fashion, giving revelations about the future (or heavenly) realm, which is depicted in sharp contrast to the present corrupt age. On the other hand, Revelation also presents itself as a gentler literary type—an epistle addressed to seven Asian Christian congregations in prominent towns near Ephesus. Paul's letters are the antecedent of this epistolary form of communications in the early church. This practice possibly influenced the writer of Revelation to employ this genre, an apocalyptic letter, while living in a time of vicious and intense persecution.

The solemn opening of the letter reaches its climax in Revelation 1:8 with a self-revelatory statement by God, a statement ascribed to the Eternal and Almighty One which reads, "'I am the Alpha and the Omega,' says the Lord God, 'who is and who was and who is to come, the Almighty'" (ESV). Who is the Alpha and Omega mentioned in Scripture? This term "Alpha and Omega" is only mentioned three times in the entire Bible, and we find all three instances in the book of Revelation: 1:8; 21:6; and 22:13. *Alpha* and *Omega* are the first and last letters of the Greek alphabet. These references to the first and last letters of the Greek alphabet symbolize God's role as the one who exclusively exists at the beginning and end of all time. Alpha and Omega affirm and declare the totality and completeness of the Divine Being's boundless life, which embraces all while transcending all.

God is the complete all-encompassing and eternal one, the source and finality of all things as referenced in Isaiah 44:6. In that passage it is contended that the Lord—Israel's King—and His redeemer, the Lord of Hosts, says, "I am the first and I am the last; and beside me there is no God." To speak of God as the Alpha and the Omega does not necessitate restricting God to only the beginning and the end. Still, it is to proclaim the all-inclusive entirety of God's sovereignty and power. God does not just rule the beginning and the end of history, but all that lies in between as well. Thus, our God's formulation as the Alpha and Omega sets the context for the entire book—for God is the beginning and the end.

The writer of Revelation employs a courageous choice of words for that time—for to make a public profession of faith in Jesus Christ could potentially place one in grave danger of, at the least, becoming a social and commercial outcast or, at worst, being legally murdered as an enemy of the well-known Roman empire. John himself was on Patmos's prison island as he wrote (and prison islands were not merely places of incarceration; usually, they were holding cells for those awaiting execution). In Revelation's poetic language that is described as "apocalyptic," John captured the awful conditions as they existed in his day and was convinced that they were God's adjudication upon a world gone wrong. He described the devastation of the forces of nature run amok; he witnessed the moral corruption that turns humans into beasts and destroys society from within; he saw the catastrophic results of violent conflict. Yet, through all of this, the writer declares that God is the Beginning and the End, the one "who is and who was and who is to come." In the final analysis, God is sovereign over all things. Nothing happens outside of God's sovereignty, and in the end, our Almighty God will fulfill, complete, and accomplish His good purposes for His glory and for our blessing.

The second clause of verse 8 employs a wordplay that sets God in contrast to imperial rule and Rome's power: the emperor was commonly called autocrator or self-ruler. Here, God, the Almighty, is called *Pantocrator*, which means "ruler of all." The emphasis in this title is that God is the supreme ruler. For John's readers, such an affirmation would have been a powerful encouragement. In the minds of many Christians, the Roman rulers, political systems, and institutions appeared to be the ones who were in charge, the "almighty ones." While the Roman emperor would have seen himself as all-powerful, the text affirms that God is the truly almighty one. In Revelation 22:13 (ESV), Christ says, "I am the Alpha and the Omega, the first and the last, the beginning and the end." These descriptive expansions explain the meaning of "Alpha and Omega." God is the one who was "in the beginning" (Genesis 1:1) and who will be at the end. All creation owes its existence to God, so all creation finds its ultimate meaning and purpose in God. Creation and eschatology are united in God. What God began in creation, God will bring to completion at the Eschaton—the last days.

In his eloquent meditation on Revelation entitled *Reverse Thunder*, Eugene Peterson offers this insight: "People who live by faith have an acute sense of living 'in the middle.' We believe that God is at the beginning of all things, and we believe that God is, after all, life. We assume that the beginning was good. It is agreed that the conclusion will be good. We begin the first chapter knowing there is a final chapter." Therefore, we do not lose heart. Our God is the Alpha and the Omega, the one who is and was and is to come. He is the Almighty. Knowing and believing this about God is indeed a source of hope and comfort for Christians in every age until Jesus Christ returns.

THE GREAT HYMN
PASS ME NOT O GENTLE SAVIOR

Pass me not, O gentle Savior
Hear my humble cry
While on others Thou art calling
Do not pass me by
Savior, Savior
Hear my humble cry
While on others Thou art calling
Do not pass me by

Let me at Thy throne of mercy
Find a sweet relief
Kneeling there in deep contrition
Help my unbelief
Savior, Savior
Hear my humble cry
While on others Thou art calling
Do not pass me by

Trusting only in Thy merit
Would I seek Thy face
Heal my wounded, broken spirit
Save me by Thy grace
Savior, Savior
Hear my humble cry
While on others Thou art calling
Do not pass me by

DR. E. DEWEY SMITH JR.
House of Hope Atlanta
Decatur, Georgia

DR. E. DEWEY SMITH JR.
HOUSE OF HOPE ATLANTA
DECATUR, GEORGIA

JESUS IS THE AUTHOR AND FINISHER

Hebrews 12:1-4

1 Wherefore seeing we also are compassed about with so great a cloud of witnesses, let us lay aside every weight, and the sin which doth so easily beset us, and let us run with patience the race that is set before us,

2 Looking unto Jesus the author and finisher of our faith; who for the joy that was set before him endured the cross, despising the shame, and is set down at the right hand of the throne of God.

3 For consider him that endured such contradiction of sinners against himself, lest ye be wearied and faint in your minds.

4 Ye have not yet resisted unto blood, striving against sin.

THE GREAT HYMN
DOWN AT THE CROSS

Down at the cross
Where my savior died
Down where for cleansing
From sin I cried
There to my heart
Was the blood applied
Glory to His name

I am so wondrously
Saved from my sin
Jesus so sweetly
Abides within
There at the cross
Where He took me in
Glory to His name

Singin' glory to His name
Glory to His name
There to my heart was the blood applied
Glory to His name
Oh, precious fountain that saves from sin
I am so glad I have entered in
There Jesus saves me and keeps me clean
Glory to His name
Singin' glory to His name
Glory to His name
There to my heart was the blood applied
Glory to His name

Come to this fountain so rich and sweet
Cast thy poor soul at thy savior's feet
Plunge in today
You'll be made complete
Glory to His name
I'm singin' glory to His name
Glory to His name
There to my heart was the blood applied
Glory to His name

Lord, today I approach You, knowing that there are times in life when You graciously grant me the privilege of a new beginning. There are even seasons when You permit me the blessing of doing some things over. Lord, my prayer right now is for You to take my life and write a new chapter in the book of my journey on earth. Delete the errors of my way, destroy satanic setbacks, and do away with anything or anybody that distracts me from You. In the name of Jesus I pray. Amen.

Article 21

THE GREAT HIM
JESUS IS THE AUTHOR AND FINISHER
Hebrews 12:1-4

by
Dr. E. Dewey Smith Jr.

In the eighth century BC, the first recorded Olympic Games were held. Every four years, representatives of Greek city-states would gather at Mount Olympus for athletic competition. The various competitions convened to honor Greek gods and goddesses. Mount Olympus was the acclaimed home of Greek deities. Although there was a plethora of Greek gods and goddesses, Zeus was considered the father of all deities. It was widely held that the winners of these various athletic competitions would bring honor to the gods or goddesses whom the winning contestants worshipped. Each Olympiad, citizens of Greek city-states anxiously anticipated homage being bestowed upon Zeus, Hera, Poseidon, Demeter, Athena, Apollo, Artemis, Ares, Hephaestus, Aphrodite, Hermes, and Hestia/Dionysus.

With Mount Olympus as the likely context, the writer of Hebrews pens this missive. For two thousand years, scholars have debated the identity of the author of Hebrews. St. Paul has widely been attributed authorship; however, Barnabas, Aquila, Priscilla, and Apollos are often mentioned as possible penmen. Even though the authorship of Hebrews is inconclusive, the book's inspiration continues to lift spirits, empower souls, and encourage the worship of God. Using the metaphor of athletics and the ancient Olympiads, the Hebrews writer teaches us that we are not battling or "competing" in isolation. The author instructs us about the help we have from "the grandstand" in Hebrews 12:1: "Wherefore seeing we also are compassed about with so great a cloud of witnesses." In the same way that citizens thought the Greek Empire would gather to cheer on their favorite athletes, we are reminded that we have "witnesses" who "compass" us. This means that we have the testimonies and examples of those "heroes" and "sheroes" of faith who have served before us and now empower us by their previous lives of faith. Hebrews 11 gives us a litany of saints whose stories and victories are now indelibly affixed in the "grandstands." Whenever we need visuals and examples of victory, we can look into the faith "grandstands" for encouragement.

The author of the book of Hebrews offers us help and shares what can hinder our efforts: weight and sin. We have to rid ourselves of these hindrances by "laying aside every weight, and the sin which doth so easily beset us" (verse 1). As a former athlete, I often wore ankle weights. I would walk around daily with five-pound weights around my ankles because they helped me develop speed, quickness, and explosiveness. However, on the day of competition, I could not compete with the weights on my ankles; I had to remove them to be victorious. The same principle applies to contestants on this spiritual journey. We can never be successful if we are bombarded by unnecessary "weight" and "sin." Self-evaluations are necessary as we grow, mature, and excel in all areas of our lives, after which we must rid ourselves of anything and anyone that hinders us.

After mentioning our help and hindrances, the writer admonishes us to have heart. He states in Hebrews 12:1 that we should "run with patience the race that is set before us." The Greek word for "race" in this passage is *agon*. *Agon* is where the English word *agony* is derived. This word is a reminder that as we seek to glorify our God and run our races, we must keep in mind that the Christian race is not a dash or sprint but, rather, is an agonizing marathon. Great athletes from antiquity to post-modernity can be placed in one of two categories: those who have "heart" and those who do not. In this context, the heart is not a reference to a bodily organ but, rather, to tenacity, perseverance, and toughness. One of the most significant accolades athletes can receive is that they have "heart." As Christians, we should strive to possess and demonstrate "heart" by enduring and maintaining when times get tough.

Hebrews 12:1-2 opens with an emphasis on our help, hindrances, and heart—but closes with HIM: "Looking unto Jesus the author and finisher of our faith; who for the joy that was set before him endured the cross, despising the shame, and is set down at the right hand of the throne of God" (verse 2). Ancient athletes at Mount Olympus maintained a focus on their Greek deities as they were competing. Their ultimate aim was to bring reverential adoration to a pagan god or goddess. In the most brutal battles, they would gain strength from thoughts of making their personal god/goddess preeminent. Each contestant believed that their deity commenced the match, but these same contestants were in a theological quandary when they were not victorious in the end.

This passage reminds us that we should always keep our focus on Jesus of Nazareth. Unlike the Greek godhead, Jesus not only authors the faiths of believers but finishes them without fail. While "the twelve Olympians" of the Greek pantheon could start but not always finish, Jesus

Christ specializes in "finishing." Theologically speaking, He never starts until He finishes. In the plan of the Divine, God always finishes and then backs up to start. Jesus, "who for the joy that was set before him endured the cross, despising the shame" (verse 2b), could do this because of what had been determined before His race ever began. Before Christ ever came from Glory and made it to Jerusalem, "joy" had been set before Him. Jesus was co-existent with the Creator, yet His first act was not creation. Christ's initial affinity with a "garden" was not the one in Eden but, rather, in Gethsemane. In the realm of the Divine, Jesus had been slain before "the foundations of the world." Jesus did not create and then save; He saved and then decided to create. We can always look to Jesus because what He authors is finished before it was authored.

May we forever be resolute as we look to HIM! May our trust perpetually be in HIM! May we hope in HIM! May we believe in HIM! May we honor HIM! May we obey HIM! May we worship HIM! May we lift HIM! May we represent HIM! May we forever be with HIM.

THE GREAT HYMN
JUST AS I AM

Just as I am, without one plea
But that Thy blood was shed for me
And that Thou bid'st me come to Thee
O Lamb of God, I come! I come

Just as I am, though tossed about
With many a conflict, many a doubt
Fighting and fears within without
O Lamb of God, I come, I come

Just as I am, and waiting not
to rid my soul of one dark blot
to thee whose blood can cleanse each spot
O Lamb of God, I come, I come

Just as I am, poor, wretched, blind
Sight, riches, healing of the mind
Yea, all I need, in Thee to find
O Lamb of God, I come, I come!

Just as I am, Thou wilt receive
Wilt welcome, pardon, cleanse, relieve
Because Thy promise I believe
O Lamb of God, I come, I come
Because Thy promise I believe
O Lamb of God, I come, I come

DR. MELVIN V. WADE SR.
Mount Moriah Baptist Church
Los Angeles, California

DR. MELVIN V. WADE, SR.
MOUNT MORIAH BAPTIST CHURCH
LOS ANGELES, CALIFORNIA

JESUS IS THE SAVIOR

Matthew 1:18-21

18 Now the birth of Jesus Christ was on this wise: When as his mother Mary was espoused to Joseph, before they came together, she was found with child of the Holy Ghost.

19 Then Joseph her husband, being a just man, and not willing to make her a public example, was minded to put her away privily.

20 But while he thought on these things, behold, the angel of the LORD appeared unto him in a dream, saying, Joseph, thou son of David, fear not to take unto thee Mary thy wife: for that which is conceived in her is of the Holy Ghost.

21 And she shall bring forth a son, and thou shalt call his name JESUS: for he shall save his people from their sins.

THE GREAT HYMN
JESUS, JESUS, JESUS

Jesus, Jesus, Jesus; there's just something about that name.
Master, Savior, Jesus, like the fragrance after the rain;
Jesus, Jesus, Jesus, let all Heaven and earth proclaim
Kings and kingdoms will all pass away,
But there's something about that name.
Kings and kingdoms will all pass away,
But there's something about that name.

O Lord, our Lord, how excellent is Thy name in all the earth! Your name is great. Your name is wonderful. Your name is mighty! In Your name is healing, hope, salvation, and strength. Through Your name come heaven's authority, divine ability, and a complete sense of spiritual adequacy. Thank You, Jesus, for who You are to us. Please, Lord, I ask just this one petition of You: cause me to live in a way each day that brings honor and glory to Your name. In the name of Jesus I pray. Amen.

Article 22

THE GREAT HIM
JESUS IS THE SAVIOR
Matthew 1:18-21

"THE MATCHLESS NAME OF JESUS"

by
Dr. Melvin V. Wade Sr.

It very often happens that a name given to a man can be a one-word summary of who a man is and/or what a man has done. A name was often descriptive of some unique characteristic feature of a person. It is so with the names of Alexander the Great, William the Conqueror, Ivan the Terrible, Bloody Mary, John the Baptist, and Simon the Zealot. And this fact is especially true when it comes to Jesus, for the nomenclature *Jesus* is a one-word summary of who He is and what He is to the world. In the Bible days, at times, names were messages from God to His people. It proved to be true with the names of Hosea's children. Their names were messages to Israel because of their backslidden condition—their idolatrous, adulterous behavior.

In 1 Samuel 4, Eli's dying daughter-in-law gave birth to a son and named him Ichabod, suggesting that God and His glory were gone from Israel. And the same is true with the name of Jesus, for God's ultimate message is in Jesus' name. When a man's character believed or gave a false impression of his name in the Bible, the name was changed. It happened to Abraham, Sarah, Jacob, Peter, and Paul. But not so with Jesus. There is what is called "The Doctrine of Impeccability." This means that it was impossible for Jesus to sin. The reason is that Jesus was virgin-conceived, and He got sinless blood from the Holy Spirit. Therefore, Jesus needed no name change. Why is the name *Jesus* matchless?

Its Derivation
The name *Jesus* is matchless because of the source from whence it was derived. Jesus got His name from God, the Father, the God who is real; the God who is Adorned in Authority, Girdled in Grace, Mantled in Majesty, Robed in Righteousness, Vested in Virtue, Glorious in His Grace, Judicious in His Justice, Kind in Kingliness, Limitless in Lordship, Magnificent in His Majesty, Matchless in Mercy—the God who has a voluntary relationship with everything, but

has no necessary relationship to anything or anyone named His *sui generis* Son, Jesus. Even though God allows man to work in divine/ human cooperation with Him, there are some things that only God is able to handle. There are some areas that God keeps exclusive to Himself. First, there are some areas that God keeps exclusive to Himself because man is sinful, and whatever man touches, he leaves the taint of sin on it. And there are some things that the Lord does not want tainted; therefore, He does not allow man to put his tainted hands on those things. Consequently, He prohibits man. And God has kept to Himself the naming of Jesus.

Second, there are some things that only an omnipotent, omniscient, and omni-sapient God can handle. And it is an axiomatic, indubitable, irrefragable fact that God is able. That's why Paul writes in Ephesians 3:20, "Now unto him that is able to do exceeding abundantly above all that we can ask or think . . . ." So, this God, who is free from sin and tainting—this God, who is exceedingly Able—is responsible for naming His only begotten, one-of-a-kind Son. The name *Jesus* is above every name. Second, it is because of . . .

Its Definition
The name *Jesus* means "Jehovah is Salvation." What this says is that Jesus is what He is called—for Jesus is Salvation. In looking at the definition of the name *Jesus*, we see that Jesus is not only exalted in nature, but He is exalted in purpose. We are living at a time when men are seeking to de-divinize Jesus. They seek to strip Him of His deity. When we listen to some people, they seek to tell us what sort of man Jesus was. But the issue is not what sort of Man He is, but who is He. In Philippians 2:6, Paul writes, "Who, being in the form of God . . . ." The phrase "being in the form of God" tells us that Jesus is equal to God the Father. Jesus, confessing the truth of Himself, said, "I and my Father are one." There are two theological words. One is *Perichoresis*, and the other is *Circumincession*. These words describe and speak of the binding relationship of the Trinity. Jesus said, "I am in the Father and the Father in Me." Jesus' name not only tells of His nature, but it also tells of His purpose. His purpose is "Shall Save." The words "Shall Save" have reference to the idea of deliverance and rescuing. And the purpose of Jesus is to rescue and deliver the called of God from the deadly pollution of sin. Finally, it is matchless because of . . .

Its Doxology
Paul says, "That at the name of Jesus every knee should bow, . . . and that every tongue should confess that Jesus Christ is Lord, to the glory of God the Father" (Philippians 2:10, 11). Look at the fact that when Jesus came the first time in His kenosis or incarnation, He met with

degradation and utter humiliation. The world did not recognize or receive Him. He was despised and rejected by men. He was accused of being an illegitimate child. He was said to be insane, working by the power of Beelzebub. But Jesus promised, after His resurrection and ascension, that He is coming back again. And when He comes again, He will not be the humiliated Jesus, but He will be the exalted Christ. He will wear a crown of Glory and Power. He will be shrouded in Judgment regalia. He will come as a commander-in-chief of a vast army. When He comes again, it will be a time of accounting and not continuing opportunity. When He comes again, all will submit, all will confess, all will bow, but not all will be saved. For the rejected, bowing will be painful—but it will be blissful joy for the acceptors.

THE GREAT HYMN
HE LOOKED BEYOND MY FAULTS

Amazing Grace shall always be my song of praise
For it was grace that brought me liberty
I do not know just why He ever came to love me so
He looked beyond my faults and saw my need
And I shall forever lift mine eyes to Calvary
To view the cross where Jesus died for me
How marvelous the grace that caught my falling soul
He looked beyond my faults and saw my need
I shall forever lift mine eyes to Calvary
To view the cross where Jesus died for me

How marvelous the grace that caught my falling soul

He looked beyond my faults and saw my needs

He looked beyond my faults and saw my needs

PASTOR MARVIN L. SAPP
Chosen Vessel Church
Fort Worth, Texas

PASTOR MARVIN L. SAPP
CHOSEN VESSEL CHURCH
FORT WORTH, TEXAS

JESUS IS THE CHRIST

Matthew 16:16-18

16 And Simon Peter answered and said, Thou art the Christ, the Son of the living God.

17 And Jesus answered and said unto him, Blessed art thou, Simon Barjona: for flesh and blood hath not revealed it unto thee, but my Father which is in heaven.

18 And I say also unto thee, That thou art Peter, and upon this rock I will build my church; and the gates of hell shall not prevail against it.

THE GREAT HYMN
JESUS IS ALL THE WORLD TO ME

Jesus is all the world to me:
My life, my joy, my all.
He is my strength from day to day;
Without Him I would fall.
When I am sad, to Him I go;
No other one can cheer me so.
When I am sad, He makes me glad;
He's my Friend.

Jesus is all the world to me,
My Friend in trials sore.
I go to Him for blessings, and
He gives them o'er and o'er.
He sends the sunshine and the rain;
He sends the harvest's golden grain:
Sunshine and rain, harvest of grain—
He's my Friend.

Jesus is all the world to me,
And true to Him I'll be.
Oh, how could I this Friend deny
When He's so true to me?
Following Him I know I'm right;
He watches o'er me day and night.
Following Him by day and night,
He's my Friend.

Jesus is all the world to me,
I want no better friend.
I trust Him now; I'll trust Him when
Life's fleeting days shall end.
Beautiful life with such a Friend;
Beautiful life that has no end!

Lord of Heaven and Lamb of the Cross, I approach You in this petition because You are the Son of David and the root of Jesse. You are the promised Messiah, born King of the Jews and Savior of the world. You are the Christ. Lord Jesus, without You life is hopeless, but because of You, every day gets sweeter as days go by. My petition for this moment of supplication that I lay at Your feet is this: use the life You have given me to show the world what it is like to meet You. In the name of Jesus I petition heaven. Amen.

Article 23

**THE GREAT HIM
JESUS IS THE CHRIST
Matthew 16:16-18**

**by
Pastor Marvin L. Sapp**

What do you count on in life? Perhaps you count on friends and family, your job, money, or anything that makes you feel happy, safe, and successful. When you count on something or someone, expectations come along with that, whether they are right or wrong. For example, famous child actors struggle when they grow up and no longer have the appeal they had as children. These actors counted on their fans, their agents, the studio management, and the money they made. They expected this to be their life forever, but soon discovered that life could let you down.

What can we count on in a world with so much going on right now, including the pandemic, the economy, and racial unrest? To whom do we turn that can bring us through all of this? Do we count on the scientists who have created a vaccine for Covid-19? Do we count on elected officials or police officers to keep the peace and fix the economy? Perhaps if we have enough money, we can get through all of these things. On whom do we count? I believe the Bible gives a convincing answer as to whom we can count on 100 percent.

There is no leeway for letdowns. There is proof that Jesus is the one whom we can fearlessly count on at all times. The statements of what was to come came from the prophets. Prophets never had an easy life. They were God's spokespersons, and that job meant they spoke what God told them to say, to whomever He told them to say it to, at the time He told them to say it. The culture in biblical times was a little different from the time of today. In the times of kings, emperors, and pharaohs, a word from one with authority could bring death to the deliverer. But when God calls our names, following Him is advised. There are prophecies fulfilled in the life of Jesus Christ that have not been brought to pass by anyone else. Scholars profess that it is improbable that any other human in history could accomplish a small portion of these, but Jesus perfectly actualized them all.

The following are a few of the prophecies that Jesus completed, but I encourage the study of them all. It will strengthen your faith and change the way you live. Isaiah 7:14 (ASV) is a well-known verse that reads, "Therefore the Lord himself will give you a sign: behold, a virgin shall conceive, and bear a son, and shall call his name Immanuel." As with any nativity scene you see during the Christmas season, it tells you it happened. The figures that stand around the manger with the animals and hay are more than a pretty decoration. They represent the truth that Mary, a virgin, became pregnant by the Holy Spirit and gave birth to the anointed one. That's what the name *Christ* means: "anointed one." It's not Jesus' last name, but a description of who He is. He is Jesus the Christ.

The Bible also tells us of this happening in Luke 1:28a: "And the angel came in unto her, and said, Hail, thou that art highly favored, the Lord is with thee." God made that promise through His messenger Isaiah. Anyone in need of a miracle? The prophet Isaiah also spoke about how the Messiah would perform miracles. "Then the eyes of the blind shall be opened, and the ears of the deaf shall be unstopped. Then shall the lame man leap as a hart, and the tongue of the dumb shall sing; for in the wilderness shall waters break out, and streams in the desert" (Isaiah 35:5-6 ASV). This is a tall order for one person to perform, but Jesus did it all.

In Matthew 11:2-6, John the Baptist wondered if Jesus was really the one he could count on to be the Christ. While John was in prison, he sent his disciples to ask Jesus if he were the one or if someone else would be coming. Jesus told the disciples to tell John, "The blind receive their sight, and the lame walk, the lepers are cleansed, and the deaf hear, and the dead are raised up, and the poor have good tidings preached to them" (Matthew 11:5, ASV). Jesus is in the miracle business. Nothing is too hard for Him.

Of course, we need to talk about the greatest miracle of them all: raising people from the dead. "I shall not die, but I shall live, and recount the deeds of the LORD. The LORD has punished me severely, but he did not give me over to death" (Psalm 118:17-18, NRSV). Psalm 118 was written by David, who is an important part of Jesus' genealogy. The fulfillment comes many years later as some women who were supportive followers of Jesus went to the cave to anoint His body. They arrive, the stone is moved aside, but there is no Jesus. In short, His body was not present. What they see next are men in bright clothing. They are scared. In their fright, the women bow down with their faces to the ground, but the men say to them, "Why do you look for the living among the dead? He is not here; he has risen!

Remember how he told you, while he was still with you in Galilee: 'The Son of Man must be delivered over to the hands of sinners, be crucified and on the third day be raised again'" (Luke 24:5-7, NIV).

The women became the first evangelists as they went back and told the disciples what happened. Some didn't believe them, but Peter went to the tomb and saw linen strips lying on the rock. Jesus came back just like He said He would. Jesus appeared to others as well. Everything happened just as the prophets had said. Nothing was missed. Jesus is the Christ, the one that can always be counted on. He will never fail you or me.

THE GREAT HYMN
BECAUSE HE LIVES

God sent His Son, they called him Jesus,
He came to love, heal and forgive;
He lived and died, to buy my pardon,
An empty grave is there to prove my Savior lives.

Because He lives, I can face tomorrow,
Because He lives, all fear is gone;
Because I know He holds the future,
And life is worth the living just because He lives.

How sweet to hold a newborn baby,
And feel the pride, and joy he gives;
But sweeter still the calm assurance,
This child can face uncertain days because He lives.

Because He lives, I can face tomorrow,
Because He lives, all fear is gone;
Because I know He holds the future,
And life is worth the living just because He lives.

And then one day I'll cross the river,
I'll fight live's final war with pain;
And then as death gives way to victory,
I'll see the lights of glory and I'll know He lives.

Because He lives, I can face tomorrow,
Because He lives, all fear is gone;
Because I know He holds the future,
And life is worth the living just because He lives.
Eternal life, eternal joy,
He's my Friend.

CPSIA information can be obtained
at www.ICGtesting.com
Printed in the USA
BVHW010218160421
605109BV00013B/399